# Successful
# Selling

# For Small
# Business

What It Takes and How To Do It

## Jackie Wade

# eBook edition

As a buyer of the print edition of *Successful Selling for Small Business* you can now download the eBook edition free of charge to read on an eBook reader, your smart phone or your computer. Simply go to: **ebooks.brightwordpublishing.com/successfulsales** or using your smart phone, point it at the below.

You can then register and download your eBook copy of the book.

# www.brightwordpublishing.com

To Mum and Dad.
For helping me become who I am today,
thank you.

A Brightword book
www.brightwordpublishing.com


HARRIMAN HOUSE LTD
3A Penns Road
Petersfield
Hampshire
GU32 2EW
GREAT BRITAIN


Tel: +44 (0)1730 233870
Fax: +44 (0)1730 233880
Email: enquiries@harriman-house.com
Website: www.harriman-house.com

First published in Great Britain in 2012 by Harriman House.

ISBN: 978-1-908003-19-5

British Library Cataloguing in Publication Data

A CIP catalogue record for this book can be obtained from the British Library.

Design, layout and typesetting
by Mosaic (Teesdale) Ltd., Middleton-in-Teesdale.
www.mosaicprintdesign.co.uk


Printed and bound by the CPI Group (UK) Ltd, Chippenham

# Contents

# Introduction –
# Challenging Times

I have been selling since I was five years old; I can clearly remember the first shiny shilling! Interestingly no-one taught me to sell until I was almost thirty; somehow I just did it, and did it well – it came naturally and I loved it. From selling sweets in my grandmother's grocery store I progressed to running market stalls around Dublin's fair city, then moved on to the more challenging and exotic world of international business-to-business sales. I operated in many different scenarios, different languages and different cultures, selling different products and services, and yet all, somehow, were the same. It was all about connecting with the right people, in the right way, with the right story, and not giving up.

When I set up my company, 'Winning Sales', back in 2000, and began working with others to help fine-tune and improve their sales performance, I quickly understood the important dynamics of nature and nurture. For some people (the minority), selling comes naturally: it's instinctive or maybe even in their DNA. For others (the majority), sales is a cultivated or learned process which needs to be explored and understood, adapted and refined, so that it sits comfortably with their individual personality and style. Although the former may seem to be an easier route to fame and fortune, the latter can be just as effective and often produces better, more focused and consistent results. Ultimately, however, true sales success, as in any walk of life, hinges on the decision, desire and dedication to succeed and not give up whatever the pain barrier. In summary – it's all about the skill-set and the will-set!

Through my years in sales training I have also come to recognise that in many businesses, and especially in start-up ventures, the biggest barriers to sales success are actually fear, trepidation and an unease with, or real dislike of, actually having to sell. These emotions often serve not just to hinder the sale, but actually damage the ability of a business to grow. People naturally stick to the comfort zone of what they do best, and just occasionally feel the need to undertake a flurry of marketing activity in order to prime the sales pipeline.

Without a doubt, businesses today across the world face unprecedented, challenging times. We teeter on the brink of a possible 'double-dip' global recession; unemployment rises and resources are scarce. Against this backdrop, many determined, entrepreneurial people are taking greater control of their own destiny, deciding to pick up the 'start-up' gauntlet. There is for them, therefore, a greater need than ever to address the issue of proactive selling. In highly competitive marketplaces, can you realistically expect to grow a business successfully without reaching out and engaging effectively with new customers, convincing them that you are the best choice when it comes to solving their problem or need? Marketing is great, and great marketing may generate enough sales without ever needing to physically sell; however in many cases, marketing will simply drive potential customers to your door (whether that door is real or virtual) and then it's over to you and your people to ensure they buy from you and come back again and again and again. In a competitive marketplace where sellers are many and buyers are few, it is truly imperative to 'get' the principles of the sales process and be proactive in applying them. It is often not a question of the best product or service that wins the day, but rather the best seller – the one who can truly make an impact and convince potential buyers that they cannot go it alone, they need to take action and buy from them!

This short book aims to help you get comfortable with selling and sales, hopefully dispelling along the way some common misconceptions and myths around selling and sales people. It will share with you some useful tips, tools and processes that will get you started and help you recognise and avoid some common pitfalls when you're starting out. It will challenge you to focus on gaining real clarity about what you're selling, to whom, and why they might buy it and buy it from you. Ultimately, I believe this will set you on the right path for developing a successful sales habit for life and not just for now.

Have fun and share with me your thoughts, questions and feedback via:

Email: **jackie@winningsales.co.uk**

LinkedIn Group: Winning Sales

Twitter: **@winningsales**

# Part One

## Preparing To Sell

# 1

# Selling –
# Can Anyone do it?

# **10** things you should know about selling

1  Successful selling is not a black art – it's a logical process with an inevitable conclusion, based on a simple series of pre-planned, well-executed steps.

2  Sales output is related to input – you get out of it what you put in to it.

3  Selling is not marketing and marketing is not selling.

4  Telling is not selling.

5  You cannot close what's not closable.

6  No is okay; every no brings you closer to a yes.

7  Like-ability is important, but isn't everything.

8  In sales we are all equal – buyer and seller.

9  It's not about perfection, it's about doing it.

10  Sales success = mind-set + skill-set + action!

If you've bought, borrowed, been kindly gifted or otherwise acquired this book, I'm assuming that you are currently considering your next step in taking your business forward. You will have identified that sales and selling are pretty vital, if not imperative, in order to succeed and grow. The question on your mind might be whether you personally have the necessary ability and/or sufficient motivation to kick start sales in your business, or whether you need to bring in an expert? Is selling a specialist skill or can anyone do it and achieve a reasonable level of success?

The good news is that yes, anyone can sell...well almost! – once you understand what 'selling' really means, what it takes and how to do it.

# 1 Successful selling is not a black art – it's a logical process with an inevitable conclusion, based on a simple series of pre-planned, well-executed steps

Selling is neither an art nor a science but rather an interesting combination of the two, coupled with an occasional bit of luck. Selling is scientific in that there is a logical process involved (I call it Logical Conclusion Selling©). You, the seller, must control this process in order to ensure a sale. By learning and applying this simple process (covered in chapters 6 to 8), instead of just 'winging it', your sales results will dramatically improve.

Selling is an art because each sales situation is unique – the personalities, the people, and the passions are different every time. What makes you unique, special and memorable to your buyer? What makes your potential buyer tick? How do they prefer to do business? What buttons will you need to press? Once you start to explore and understand your personality and that of your buyer, you can learn to adapt to each sales situation and enhance your sales success.

For some, the art of selling will come naturally and easily; for others the science (or process) of selling will be more comfortable. For each of us it's about finding the right balance of the art and the science which gets you the results you want in the way that best fits your style and personality; nothing false and nothing uncomfortable – it's about finding a winning sales formula that works for you each and every time.

# 2 Sales output is related to input – you get out of it what you put in to it

Selling is a measurable, quantifiable activity. The output is dependent on the input, and you should be able to measure both. In other words:

> If you do **X** consistently, you should get **y**, assuming **a**, **b** and **c**.

Of course the opposite is also true: If you don't do x, or don't do it consistently, then you won't get y!

Selling is still, to a certain extent, a numbers game, although a focus on quality and not just quantity is highly recommended for achieving the maximum return on the time you invest in the process. The basic laws of averages and probability apply; i.e., the more frequently you connect with quality prospects, the greater the chance of a positive outcome. Sitting, waiting and hoping that the world will beat a path to your door is naïve, costly and a plan unlikely to succeed. If you put the effort in and take action, you'll get the output you deserve; if you don't, you won't!

# 3 Selling is not marketing and marketing is not selling

Now is not the time for big lectures or fancy definitions in relation to sales and marketing. Simply recognise that effective marketing will help identify and attract a potential customer's interest but on its own marketing may not result in a sale (obviously in internet selling where there is no seller involvement, different rules may apply). Selling is the transactional side of marketing – it's what brings the money in. Investing in marketing without considering the sales, or conversion, process, is akin to flushing money down the drain. Real return on your marketing investment requires a robust sales process, and positive, proactive sales people (or person) focused on converting marketing-generated interest into a purchase. Marketing can be vanity, sales are sanity, and repeat business is king!

# 4 Telling is not selling

Finding potential customers and telling them what you do is not selling – that's dumping information on them, or what I call 'the vomit sell' – a real turn-off. The good news is you don't have to have the 'gift of the gab' to sell successfully, in fact this can be a real barrier. You need to learn to 'zip your lips' and listen. Some of the key skills you need to develop to be an effective seller are:

- questioning skills in order to explore your customer's needs (page 79)

- listening skills (page 83) in order to understand what your customer is saying (and not saying)

- matching skills (page 86) in order to tailor your particular product or service to each unique sales situation and customer.

## 5 You cannot close what's not closable

When we talk about naturally gifted sales people, we often say things like 'they could sell ice to the Eskimos' or 'oil to the Arabs'. Behind this lies the mistaken belief that great selling means you could sell something to someone even if they didn't want or need it. True, there are some people who could do this but is this the kind of business you are trying to build? This is short-term gain and long-term pain, with the resulting risk of an annoyed customer, no repeat business and a negative reputation.

The real skill in selling is the ability to match your solution to the customer's need. You are out there as a 'match maker', identifying customers who have needs for which you have the perfect solution, or at least a solution better than the alternatives. If your proposed solution – product or service – doesn't fit, or if the customer believes it doesn't fit, then no amount of cajoling or sales banter will result in a happy customer. Maybe you'll get the initial 'forced' sale in a few instances, but you won't get repeat business or referrals.

## 6 No is okay; every no brings you closer to a yes

Start embracing, even enjoying no, telling yourself that, with another no out of the way, yes must be just around the corner! Once you decide to get proactive and not sit back and wait for business to come to you, it's inevitable that the outcome will be a few people saying no. The inescapable truth is that not everyone out there needs you, just some people, some of the time, and that's fine. Your challenge is to manage no and focus on getting to yes. Every single no is taking you one step closer to that vital yes. Remember, too, that rejection isn't personal and that even the best sales people get their fair share of no's, so embrace them, learn from them and move on...quickly! The alternative is to sit and wait...and wait...and wait.

## 7 Like-ability is important, but isn't everything

You'll no doubt have heard a million times that we buy from people we like, and I would certainly agree; being likeable certainly helps the seller during the sales process and being unlikeable, or an ass, doesn't. We most definitely decline, or even refuse, to buy from people we don't like unless there is no other option (and even then, as soon as a better option presents itself, we're off to greener pastures!).

So, getting back to like-ability, it helps but it's not everything. Many sales people and non-sales people alike make the mistake of relying purely on personality to win business. This does work sometimes, but not always, and certainly not as much in challenging market conditions as during a 'boom' economy. People buy with their hearts and with their heads (the purchase is emotional as well as logical) and the truly good sales person understands both these aspects. As explained in number 1 above, the selling process has to lead to a logical outcome in order for the buyer to take action. Your job is to help that buyer get to the logical outcome and not just rely on them liking you and so buying from you. Indeed, I would say that one of the most common mistakes in selling is to interpret getting on well with someone during a sales meeting as a buying signal and to go away expecting the phone to ring – it won't, you need process and closure.

## 8  In sales we are all equal – buyer and seller

You are you – fabulous, wonderful you – inventor, engineer, entrepreneur, techno-guru, life coach... You believe you have something great and of value – your product, your service, and you.

Your buyer is equally special – not better, not greater, not more important. They may drive a faster car, have a bigger house or make millions of pounds, but you're still both equal.

This mind-set is important in sales. You are not less than, inferior, the underdog, or 'the sales-rep' – you are equal. To succeed in sales, you will need to remind yourself of this and not feel that you are unworthy. If you believe you have something of value which would meet a potential buyer's need (a need which might not yet be obvious to the buyer), then brilliant, bring it on! Believe that you can connect as equals. Beware, too, of falling into the opposite trap, that is of being arrogant or cocky and believing that you know what's best for your customer. You cannot possibly know this, and this attitude will not win you any favours, but only serve to alienate a potential customer.

## 9  It's not about perfection, it's about doing it

To sell well, you don't have to get it perfect at first – just do it. Doing it reasonably well is better than not doing it all, or sitting on the fence waiting for the phone to ring. The worst thing that can happen if you try and don't succeed is that you'll actually learn something. You will only get better through practice. In my experience, buyers often prefer 'less than perfect' sales people. If the seller appears too slick and confident then the buyer can feel threatened or repelled. People often act on instinct to help the rookie, the more natural (less 'salesy') person, or someone who doesn't appear to know it all. Of course, learn the basics before you get started, so you don't waste your time and energy, but then get going and review, fine-tune and improve as you go along. Too much theory and not enough practice is not a good thing. Read this book, do it, read it again and then do it better, until it becomes second nature.

# 10 Sales success = mind-set + skill-set + action!

To achieve sales success, you will require a mixture of the right mind-set, a simple but successful sales process (or structure) and the commitment to doing it, that is taking action. Sometimes, but not always, an unknown but not extraordinary quantity of luck will also help.

Neither mind-set nor skill-set in isolation will be enough.

Once you get the balance of this formula right and the principles and techniques embedded in your psyche, the trick is to keep applying and adapting it over and over again. Steady business growth requires a consistent and concerted level of sales activity, otherwise any success will be short-lived.

# 2

# A Simple Sales Framework – the Vital Ingredients

For those new to sales, let's start with a quick overview of what selling is all about.

## Making connections

First and foremost, the sales process is simply about connecting the **right** people, in the **right** way, with the **right** solution. The emphasis clearly is on the word '**right**'; if any one element of the process is 'wrong', then the outcome will be wrong, too, that is it won't work and it won't result in a successful sale.

## Demonstrating value

Next, the process needs to demonstrate or communicate one or more clear benefits or aspects of value to the potential buyer so that it's obvious your product or service is right for them. Make this a 'no-brainer'.

## Helping them take the leap

Then crucially, it's about facilitating change – helping the buyer to take action – and with you!

If it helps, think of moving your customer from place A (without you and your product) to place B (with you and your product). Place B must be a significantly better place than place A, otherwise there is no reason for them to move from one to the other. (We revisit this concept in chapter 4 when we explore the benefit and value of your product.) The better that place B is, the easier and more logical it is for the potential customer to take action and buy; it's Logical Conclusion Selling©. If the attraction of place B is not sufficiently compelling, then they will stay put in place A (maintaining the status quo) as it's easier.

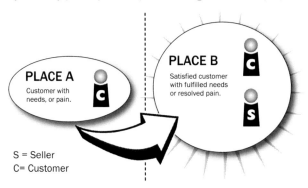

PLACE A
Customer with needs, or pain.

PLACE B
Satisfied customer with fulfilled needs or resolved pain.

S = Seller
C= Customer

## Once is never enough

And finally it's about doing all of the above consistently and repeatedly, not just willy-nilly, on an ad hoc basis, or when you have the time.

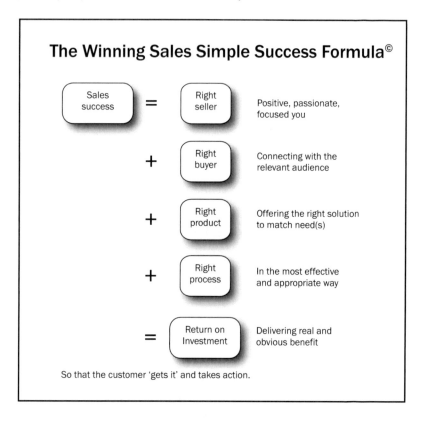

This formula for successful selling is truly a case of the sum of the parts working together to bring you optimum results, rather than any one element being critical on its own.

## The whole process and nothing but the whole process

You can have an amazing product or service but it will not sell itself. Unless you actually reach out and seek to engage with people who have a need for what you're offering, either now or in the future, it will never sell. No amount of sitting and waiting for the phone to ring or for the customer to come knocking at your door will change this.

Equally, you may have done great research, identified your perfect audience (who, in your mind, quite justifiably needs your product or service) and even made the initial connection. However, unless and until you can effectively get across to that potential buyer why they should bother with you, and create obvious and real benefit in their mind, they will not move to buy: zero action, no sale!

Also critical is your timing, planning and persistence. It is the steady and continuing engagement with enough qualified prospects which will allow you to develop an ongoing level of sales such that your growth is consistent and dependable, rather than erratic and unreliable.

Over the next few chapters, we will delve into each of these critical elements of the winning formula in more depth, developing an understanding of why getting each bit right is so vital and critical to your success. The sales process should be a logical journey for the seller as well as for the buyer: it has a start, a middle and an end, as well as a before and an after. Setting off on this journey and ensuring you and your customer get to the right destination together is all about following this road map and carefully reading the signs along the way. There may be some diversions, distractions or obstacles en route, but you must not be deterred. You must have a clear vision of this final, desirable destination and have total belief in the value of taking your customer on this journey with you. You both ultimately stand to gain significantly.

Now it's over to you, to take control and make this happen.

## Chapter overview

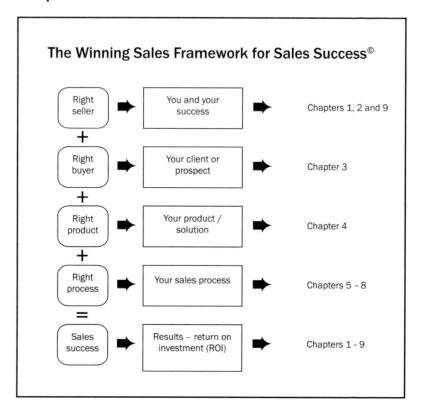

# 3

# Who Will Buy?

In this chapter we will focus on the buyer, customer or prospect. I'll share four basic rules that will help you prepare for selling to this person and achieve maximum results:

rule 1: always seek to see things from your (potential) customer's perspective

rule 2: commit to allocating specific time and effort to developing new business

rule 3: clearly identify the right person to speak to

rule 4: focus on your (potential) customer's needs.

## Rule 1: Always seek to see things from your (potential) customer's perspective

**It's about them, not you. Always think about sales and selling from your customer's or prospect's point of view – not yours!**

One of the most common pitfalls made by people trying to sell is to be too seller- or self-focused. Too frequently they use the language of 'my product', 'my service', 'me', and 'I'. As entrepreneurs, business owners, inventors and otherwise creative people, we come up with an idea, concept, product or service and believe it's brilliant (or at least hope it is)! So then we want to tell the world all about it and how great it is, assuming that everyone will want to buy it! There is often the mistaken belief that 'telling is selling' – that if we TELL enough people about what WE DO, then someone, somewhere will buy. Unfortunately, this is not necessarily true!

Yes, of course you **should** believe in yourself and your product or service – your passion and belief are vital to your success – but simply telling people what you do, however passionately you do it, is often not enough. The worst, and commonly stereotyped, sales people are often arrogant, egotistical and self-centred. Ultimately they turn customers off as they talk relentlessly about themselves. Even some of the nicest 'sales people' make the same 'telling' mistake unintentionally. They get in front of a prospective customer and just off-load or dump information. Sometimes this is the consequence of nerves, sometimes it's unbridled passion, sometimes it's that they're in a rush to get in and out as quickly as possible so as not to 'waste' the buyer's time.

To sell effectively you need to be truly **buyer-focused**; everything else must come second. Take time to focus on your potential customer or prospect as an individual, rather than simply rushing towards the sale. This approach will allow you to best match your product or service to each situation and so get maximum results. This is more than just a simple market research exercise; it's about gaining a true understanding of your potential buyer and their needs and motivations. This need to focus on the prospect applies throughout the entire sales process and will help you to significantly maximise each situation, in terms of opening the door, getting the first sale, identifying future sales and opportunities and generating referrals and other contacts. It's about taking the time to drill down rather than just skimming the surface; it's about truly connecting with your buyer by listening to them in order to understand the full extent of their needs.

## So who is your prospect or potential customer?

Throughout your business journey, you will be selling to different types of people, all with different levels of interest in you and your product – from those who are blissfully unaware to those who are committed loyal fans. I call this the spectrum of interest, and the movement along it, the 'stranger to lover syndrome': the process of moving prospects from being total strangers (unaware of the benefits your product or service would bring them), to acquaintances (casually aware of them), to friends (who know what you and your product would do for them, and like this), and ultimately to lovers (who know, love and trust your product and even rave about it).

You may, at different times, be selling to any or all of the following:

- **New prospects** – people who you believe have a need you can fulfil. They may not actually agree with you on this – at least not yet. On my 'stranger to lover' spectrum, these are for the most part strangers or acquaintances, but nonetheless, potential future loyal customers, or 'lovers'.

  Your objective is to make the initial connection or introduction and explore need.

- **Customers** – past or present customers with further requirements or needs for more of the same or other new or additional products or services. These will vary from passionate loyal fans ('lovers and friends') to more fickle, perhaps casual, 'acquaintances'.

Your objective is to stay in touch, protect and nurture them and identify new opportunities and possibilities.

- **Promoters** – people in your circle who know, like and trust you and who can lead their contacts and customers to you or you to them. They believe you can fulfil their customer's needs and are happy to recommend or connect you together. For example, a bank manager may be a 'promoter' of someone selling accountancy or book-keeping related services.

  Your objective is to maximise on your network and seek to gain warm leads and referrals.

If you are starting a business from scratch, you may be thinking of, or indeed need to, engage with 'strangers'. However, don't overlook potential promoters, friends or 'lovers' in your circle, who are extremely valuable and who can double, treble, or maybe even quadruple your 'sales force' either informally or formally. These people represent an easy, safe and often untapped way of generating warm leads – those which can be readily converted into sales.

As your business develops and grows, your sales challenge will be to time-manage your multiple relationships, striking an important balance between seeking and finding new customers, and nurturing and minding existing ones.

# Your sales challenge depends on your target audience

## New customers

## Your challenge

**Suspects** — someone you *think* might have a need for your product or service.

Don't waste time. Establish if this relationship is viable or not, 'qualify' it, and move on.

**Prospects** - someone you *know* to have a need for your product or service.

Connect with ⋯→ Engage ⋯→ Manage ⋯→ Close ⋯→ Nurture. Focus on moving prospects from cool to hot. Gain access to cold prospects via warm or hot prospects.

[Prospects might be *hot* (very interested), *warm* (open to dialogue and positive), *cool* (showing mild to little interest) or *cold* (no successful contact yet).]

## Existing customers

## Your challenge

**Active** customers – those who currently buy from you.

Don't make assumptions. Do they really know everything you do? Maximise on LTV (Lifetime Value – the value of a customer to a business over the lifetime of that active relationship). Cross-sell, upsell, gain referrals, build relationship.

**Lapsed** customers – those who have previously bought from you, but are not doing so now.

Why are they no longer buying? Have they gone elsewhere or just gone to sleep? Why?

Don't assume they have gone forever. How can you win them back or reactivate them?

## Promoters

## Your challenge

Introducers or middlemen – someone who can connect you to your potential customers; also 'warm prospects' but with a relationship or history.

Think of the big picture. Who knows you? Who could help? Don't overlook family, friends, previous colleagues, the pub, golf course, and at the school gates. Don't be shy – ask for connections. Don't overlook or forget. Seek quick wins.

Formal (incentivised) or informal (not incentivised) introducers.

# Rule 2: Commit to allocating specific time and effort to developing new business

**Always put *some* time aside to do *some* level of new business development activity. Never get complacent about this vital business discipline. How much time you devote to this will depend on your personal business goals, i.e., how much you want to grow, how fast and by when.**

### Pitfall 1: Taking your foot off the accelerator too quickly

Avoid a stop–start approach to new business development. Don't assume that you have enough customers for now and slow down new business development sales activity too soon. Think about business development as a pipeline and your leads as a flow through it. Things take time to develop along the 'strangers to lovers' spectrum and so a steady, continuous flow of potential buyers reaching the purchase point is what you are aiming to achieve. Avoid getting stuck because your leads have dried up.

### Pitfall 2: Neglecting newly won customers whilst searching for more

New customers are vulnerable and need lots of TLC. They represent easy added value sales at minimal effort. You've done some hard work to get them to this point, so don't waste that by letting them think you no longer want a relationship with them – they might still be easily wooed by your competitor. Think about the systems and processes you should put in place to manage and care for these customers to ensure they don't feel neglected and run off or alternatively, aren't left vulnerable to poaching.

### Pitfall 3: Putting all your eggs in one basket

Be careful at the early stage of your business about being too dependent on one big customer. You may be thrilled to have caught the big fish, but beware! It's always risky taking your eye off the pipeline while focusing on one major customer; you may lose that customer through no fault of your own, and then you're back to square one. Make sure you have an alternative 'plan B' and some other potential prospects simmering in the pipeline.

## Your target audience – where to start?

The best advice at start-up phase is to move quickly from a long list of general 'suspects' to a shorter, more focused and well-researched 'prospects' list.

Some people are unsure which sector or specific audience to target initially and try to hedge their bets by covering a very broad range of sectors, geographic areas and/or size of business. Their personal passion for their product blinds them once more into thinking that it is suitable for everyone. They end up trying to be all things to all people and the message of what need their product will fulfil becomes very blurred.

## Clarity is key

Know your audience, know their needs and know how you will best match your product or service to that specific person or sector. My advice is to try one, or possibly two, audience types initially, and then sequentially explore others. Drill down and truly evaluate the potential of each segment before moving on. Never try a bit here and a bit there, or you'll get distracted and the time you devote to selling will be used ineffectively.

Some of the targeting (or segmentation) criteria you might consider are summarised in the table below:

| Criteria for targeting | Your type of business | |
|---|---|---|
| | Business-to-Business (B2B) | Business-to-Consumer (B2C) |
| Location | Which territory is the best place to start - local, regional, national, global? | City, urban, rural, specific postcode, socio-economic status? |
| Size | By turnover, number of employees, space? | Family size? |
| Age | Length of time in business – start-ups, mature firms? | Age of individuals, family members? |
| Type | Specific sector or industry? | Family status? |
| Financial | Turnover, profitability, budget? | Income, disposable income? |
| Needs | What specific needs do they have in relation to your product or service? | |
| Alternatives, current practices | What do they currently do? Which competitors do they use? How can you improve on the status quo? | What is their current usage or habit? How would your product or service offer an improvement? |

# Rule 3: Clearly identify the right person to speak to

**Don't waste valuable sales time talking to the wrong person. They may appear to be the most obvious or interested or simply your easiest route in but they may not be in control of the buying decision and you may get stuck!**

Once you have decided on your target audience – which type of company, organisation, family, individual – you then need to consider the correct entry point, that is *who*, specifically, you will aim to connect with. This is particularly important in business-to-business sales into larger organisations, where multiple entry points are possible. Your choice of person to approach could make all the difference between success or failure in achieving a sale.

In every buying situation, you must clearly identify 'the M·A·I·N Players':

Who has the **M** oney?

Who has the **A** uthority?

Who has the **I** nfluence?

Who has the **N** eed?

Be careful not to get stuck with the person who has the tangible or active 'product need' and who has called you in. They may want and indeed need you but will they actually be able to make it happen? Can they get the money, the authority and the influencers on their side? Be clear about who is really in charge, and gain access to that person as soon as possible.

If you are selling to a small owner-managed or micro-business it is quite likely that one person assumes the roles of all the above M·A·I·N players, although there still might be influencers, such as partners, family, bank managers etc, at play.

# The decision-maker or M·A·I·N players

## Who has the Money?

Who controls the purse strings? Who has the budget for your product or service and up to what level can they sign off without needing 'a higher authority' to get involved? Have you identified this person and are they involved in your sales process? How can you get in front of them?

## Who has the Influence?

The 'influencer' is the person who, despite maybe not having the money or the authority, can influence decision-making. This may be an external consultant, an expert, a manager of another department impacted by any decision (positively or negatively), a board member, a bank manager or a friend. In any group meeting try to identify the roles of each person and be clear on who might be advising whom. Don't underestimate influencers – they can act in a positive or a negative capacity regarding decisions which will affect you.

## Who has the Authority?

This is the person who ultimately says yes or no! Are you talking to the person who has the capability of making a purchase decision in relation to your product or service? If not, how can you get that person involved directly so you are not having to work through a mediator (your message will get diluted; only do this if you have no other option). The person with authority also has the ability to 'create' money, if none is in the budget. If you can prove a Return on Investment to the person with the authority, then they can usually find the budget.

## Who has the Need?

All of the above will have different needs (tangible or intangible), motivations and agendas. Be clear on this and don't make assumptions that what is important to one person in the buying group is just as critical to someone else. (For example, your product may be great for 'the money person' and reduce production or personnel costs, however it may result in someone losing a job – which might be important to 'the influencer'.)

# M·A·I·N

## Money · Authority · Influence · Need

If you are selling to consumers, it is still worth considering the dynamics of the M·A·I·N players. A teenager might desperately want the latest Sony gizmo and the techie dad with the money may think this is a great idea. However, the mum with the final veto or authority may ultimately say no! Then Gran intervenes – the influencer!

Get to grips with the complex relationships within your decision-making group and the hierarchies of power that operate. Understand what challenges, threats and opportunities this poses for you and how it should determine your technique for closing your sale. Undertake research before your sales meeting, and probe during the meeting, to piece together this jigsaw and reveal the full picture.

# Rule 4: Focus on your (potential) customer's needs

**The key to sales success is need.**
**Focus on your customer's needs and how you can help. Your objective in effective selling is to explore needs thoroughly and then match your solution perfectly to them. Ker-ching!**

Once your approach to sales becomes proactive (where you initiate the contact) as opposed to reactive (where the customer initiates the contact), you will quickly realise that although you think, and indeed may know, that a customer needs what you have to offer, they may not always, or indeed ever, initially agree. Prospects and potential customers may not yet recognise they have a need. In sales situations, a need can either be **awake** (active) or **asleep** (dormant).

## Active need and dormant need

In the case of active need, your sales challenge is to demonstrate that your product or service is the best solution to that need, or to be the first choice. As the need is active, you don't have to convince the buyer of their need; you simply have to convince them that you are the best choice from amongst a field of possible suppliers. In this situation, being the 'best' does not equate to being the cheapest (although it might), but rather to being the best match for their needs giving them the best outcome, value for money, or Return on Investment.

In the case of dormant need, your sales challenge is to actually trigger the need, awakening a desire for something that you can supply. You can do this most effectively through questioning techniques (which we will explore more in chapter 7). This is a key skill which will move you from pushing product onto people, to leading them to explore their own needs and solutions and ultimately helping them to choose you.

For now, the key point to remember is that just because a prospect says "I don't need...", this is not a reason to give up. It simply means that they have not yet become aware of the need that you can fulfil and therefore they are not yet able to consider doing business with you.

## Need, or perceived need, lies behind every decision to buy

When you connect with a prospect, you will find them in one of the following situations:

- they are currently using a competitor's product or service to fulfil their need – so you will be offering a substitute

- they currently solve their problem or need in another way (e.g. they do it in-house) – so you will be offering an alternative

- they currently don't solve the problem at all because:

  ○ in their mind, everything's fine and they have no need – so you must highlight the need or clearly establish that things could be 'more fine'

  ○ in their mind they have 'parked their need' and decided to live with the problem for now (maybe due to a lack of budget, time, previous negative experience, etc.) – so you need to overcome barriers and offer them new options and real solutions.

In all of the above, the common theme is need. Exploring and understanding your potential customer's need is paramount to sales success.

Time invested in exploring need, either through market research (*prior* to the sales call) or through questioning technique (*during* the sales call) will be time well spent.

**Q** Why will someone **be interested** in a product or service?

**A** *Because they have a need, which concerns them, and which the relevant product or service fulfils.*

**Q** Why will someone buy a **specific** product or service?

**A** *Because they see a clear and obvious benefit to fulfilling their need with that particular product, and the benefits outweigh the cost. They are obviously 'better off' as a result of making the purchase.*

**Q** Why will someone buy that specific product **from you** rather than from someone else (assuming they know you exist)?

**A** *Because your product or service – and you – are the best fit! And you place them in a significantly better place than either doing nothing or doing it with someone else.*

## Tangible needs and intangible needs

When you are selling to an individual, think about needs in terms of both:

- tangible or physical needs (such as "I need a table to work on")

- intangible, psychological or emotional needs (such as "I need a table to work on, which is made from recycled materials and packaged and delivered in the most carbon-neutral way").

Some products simply serve a rational, physical need – it 'does what it says on the tin' – and purchases are typically price-driven. In other situations there will be more complex emotional issues at play, over which the seller has considerable influence and leverage.

*Bottled water will meet a basic need – thirst. However why will someone pay 40p for a non-branded one-litre plastic bottle from a local supermarket whereas someone else will pay £2.00+ for a smaller, specially-branded blue glass bottle from a renowned spa? More complex issues around ego, wellbeing and the environment are at play here. It's no longer simply about thirst!*

*(see Abraham Maslow's paper 'A Theory of Human Motivation')*

In business to business selling, as well as the above factors, it can serve you well to consider 'big picture' business needs, in addition to the more immediate and obvious needs. Reflect on the seven areas of business need described opposite in terms of your product or service offering. Which areas of need are the most relevant? What business needs will your product or service satisfy? These are the needs you'll seek to explore in more depth during your business meeting.

In chapter 4, we look at how you can map your product or service to the above specific types of business needs.

Before reading on, however, download and use the following template to help make sure that you understand your customer's potential needs and that you can further fine-tune your prospect target list.

 **www.winningsales.co.uk/resources**
⋯▸ Exploring Pain & Gain worksheet 1

# The seven areas of business need

| Area of business need | Considerations in relation to your product or service | Example |
|---|---|---|
| Strategic need | Does your product help a company achieve or work towards its strategic aims and objectives? | On a prospect's website, it clearly states that their business vision is to impact on 'carbon footprint'. Your company is focused on returnable packaging and has an exciting solution which can significantly reduce packaging waste. |
| Financial need | Does your product save money, improve cashflow, increase profitability, or impact in any way on the financial well-being of a business? | Your product, whilst 50% more expensive, lasts four times longer, thus increasing profits and reducing staff time wasted on the re-order process. |
| Operational need | Does your product or service enable the operational side of the business to run more smoothly, quicker, with less downtime or less hassle? | Your 24/7 service hotline guarantees a swift response to all production maintenance problems, reducing downtime by up to 50%. |
| Customer need | Does your product or service mean your prospect's customer will get a better, more efficient service, spend more, and come back more often? | Your unique marketing service offers your customers the opportunity to engage regularly and cost-effectively with their customers without leaving the office. |
| Human resources/ Staff need | Can your product or service impact positively on the well-being, productivity, retention... of your prospect's staff? | Your service focuses on significantly reducing sickness and absenteeism and getting employees happily back to the workplace. |
| Legislation/ Compliance | Will your product or service ensure your prospect can comply with the latest or anticipated legislation, industry standards, etc.? | Your product ensures small businesses have live access to the latest health and safety guidance and avoids hefty fines due to non-compliance. |
| Personal need | Is your product able to make the specific decision-maker's job or life more rewarding, easier, successful, happier...? Is there a personal, financial or other benefit to working with you? | Your service will enhance the personal health and well-being of your decision-maker. |

# 4

# Helping Your Prospect to 'Get' You

Critical to your sales success is complete clarity about what you are actually selling and the ability to convey this in a clear, precise and logical way. Of equal importance is real insight into why the customer will buy – the benefits of your product or service to them. Why is purchasing your product the most logical step for your buyer?

As mentioned in chapter 1, 'telling isn't selling', and telling someone about the features of your product or service certainly isn't the same as highlighting the benefits it will bring them. You need to consider what your focus will be, what information you should tell and how this information relates to each specific customer and each specific sales situation. Your potential customer has got to 'get it' ('it' being you and your product or service) as quickly as possible, and it needs to be blindingly obvious or else they won't buy or the purchase decision will drag on.

Too often in selling, the sales message is blurred, vague or simply packed with too much information which, whilst making perfect sense to the seller, leaves the buyer clueless or confused. The clearer the message and the more obvious the benefit, the quicker will be the result – it's logical and just makes sense. If the message is blurred and the buyer doesn't get the benefit or value, then the result will be no sale.

## **8** quick checks for your key product sales message(s)

1  Is it clear?

2  Is it short and precise?

3  Is it customer-specific?

4  Is it jargon free (i.e. easy for the customer to understand)?

5  Is it benefit-focused?

6  Is it relevant (to them, at this time, in this context)?

7  Does it add real and tangible value?

8  Is it a 'no-brainer'?

In a nutshell, is it obvious, from a customer's point of view, that buying from you or doing business with you could deliver some serious benefit for them and that they would be better off as a result? Is a purchase decision a logical and inevitable outcome?

Remember that in chapter 2 we briefly introduced the concept of moving your prospect from place A (less desirable) to place B (more desirable). Think of your prospect today, without you, in place A. Now think of your prospect tomorrow, as your customer, buying from or working with you – now they're with you in place B. Is place B an obviously better place? Can you clearly see and articulate effectively to the prospect why they should move from place A to place B – what's in it for them? If so, and they clearly get this, then there is no reason not to move and buy from you. However, if it looks and feels the same to them or only slightly different to place A where they are now, then it may suit them to just stay put and not buy (i.e. avoid change, risk, fear, time, cost...).

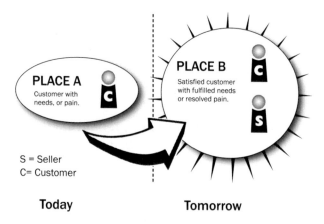

**Today**                 **Tomorrow**

To give this clarity and help get your message across effectively, there are four key areas we'll now explore:

1  What do you do...what do you *really do*?
2  How *FABulous* are you?
3  How *different* are you – what are the options or alternatives?
4  What's in it for them? What's your real *value*?

# What do you do...what do you really do?

When you think about this question, think customer! What do you do, but more importantly what do you *really* do for your customer? How does your product or service impact on their life or business? Following from the above diagram, why is place B (with you) an obviously better place than place A where they are now (without you)?

You need to ask yourself two simple questions:

- What do you **add** to your customer and their life or business?
- What do you **take away**?

Put another way, what are the customer's key gains and pains?

| Gains | Pains |
|-------|-------|
| 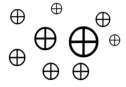 | 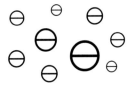 |
| Think of what you can add to your customer's life or business as the positives or the *pluses*. These are gains, benefits or advantages for them. | What you're expecting to take away from the customer are their problems, thorny issues, discomforts or the *minuses*. These are their pains. |
| Examples | Examples |
| *You help them become more profitable.* | *You take away a problem.* |
| *You make something more simple.* | *You take away a fear.* |
| *You make something run more efficiently.* | *You reduce a cost.* |
| *Your make something or someone more attractive.* | *You remove a risk.* |
| *You make life better!* | *You remove hassle.* |
| | *You lessen the load!* |

## A sales equation

$$\text{If } \sum\text{(++++)} + \sum\text{(----)} > \text{cost} = \text{ACTION!}^{©}$$

or

If the sum of the benefits added and the pains you remove is greater than the cost involved (not just the price), then there is a logical reason for the customer to take action, i.e., to buy.

If the benefit or total impact of the solution you're offering isn't obvious or if the perceived cost of using your product or service is higher in the customer's mind than the perceived benefit, then they will stay put!

Your job in sales is to get this message across as clearly as possible so that they 'get it' and want to take action – and with you!

So think carefully now about your specific customer's gains and pains.

What are the potential gains you add to your customer? What benefits does your product or service bring to them? How will their business or life be improved?

And what are the pains you can take away from your customer? What are the issues that they can resolve by using your product or service?

Download and use the templates *Exploring Pain & Gain – worksheets 1 and 2* to develop this further for your business.

**www.winningsales.co.uk/resources**
···→ Exploring Pain & Gain worksheets 1 and 2

# How FABulous are you?

Selling success depends on a blend of product, process and personal style or charisma.

## FABulous you

First, you have to believe *you* are fabulous to sell your product well. This is not being cocky or arrogant; it is simply about having internal enthusiasm, passion and confidence in what you do so that this can spread and 'infuse' potential buyers. If *you* don't believe in you and you don't manage to get this passion across, then how can you hope to get your buyer excited and enthused? In a cluttered, noisy marketplace, where so many products are perceived as 'the same', you, the seller, are the main differentiator. You simply must be fabulous. Think about it – you can differentiate your product or service on three levels:

1   The product itself.
2   The service accompanying your product.
3   The seller – **YOU**!

Your product or service may be completely unique and fabulous in itself – perhaps a new invention, a new idea, a new service. If this is the case, then wonderful and long may it last! In a global marketplace where, regardless of patents, 'copying is king', and when imitation can be regarded as a form of flattery, the length of time a product stays truly unique is short-lived.

As your competitors copy your product or service innovation, you now have to re-invent it or else consider the service offering around the product. You could provide the same product but supply it with 24/7 service, exciting packaging or amazing add-ons. Unfortunately, your competitors may also quickly follow suit.

However, and thankfully, there is one truly unique aspect to your business, and that's *you*, the seller. You are unique and fabulous. No-one can clone you and no-one can exactly replicate the make-up of your style, your approach, your personality and your individuality which you bring to every sales scenario. So be fabulous, be unique and be different. Acknowledge that in the sales process it is the sales person who can truly differentiate a product. This ability is what will help you win sales over and over again. Product or process without your personal slant is boring and scripted.

| fabulous YOU | + | right product | + | right sales process | + | right customer | ⇨ | right result (the sale) |
|---|---|---|---|---|---|---|---|---|

## FABulous selling

Second, 'FABulous' is a great way of remembering the tried and tested sales mantra of 'Features, Advantages and Benefits'.

Let me explain:

- A **feature** is quite simply an aspect of your product or service which you decide to highlight (which may or may not be unique). For example, let's imagine that you are trying to sell a drinks bottle *with a sports cap lid* – the sports cap lid in this case is a feature.

- An **advantage** is what a feature does for the customer, for example, the sports cap lid allows the customer to drink and run at the same time. This is advantageous to the customer because it allows them to do something in a better, more effective way.

- A **benefit** is the ultimate gain (or impact) for the customer of having that feature with that advantage. For example, by having a bottle with a sports cap lid, the customer can easily drink from the bottle without spillage and without having to slow down or stop. If we extend this, the ultimate benefit will be that the runner can win the race, properly hydrated, whilst not ruining their expensive T-shirt with drink stains.

Too often in sales we get hung up on features (*the sports cap lid in the case above*), and don't demonstrate tangible benefits (*winning the race, being properly hydrated and without stains on clothing*), either because we think this is obvious (it may well be to us!) or because we are so much in love with our product, or so proud of our sexy features, that we haven't actually recognised the benefits they can bring. Effective selling requires you to focus on *benefits*, not *features*, unless these are critical USPs (unique selling points/propositions) to the customer. In every case, you must make sure the customer truly recognises and 'gets' the benefits of what you can provide.

The above example also highlights that different needs and benefits are relevant to different customers. Customer X may have a problem with stained T-shirts; customer Y may have a competitive streak and a strong desire to win the race. In each sales scenario the successful sales person will highlight the particular benefits which relate to the specific pains or needs of that customer. In the case of customer X, they would describe the benefit of not ruining their expensive designer T-shirt; with customer Y they would focus on enhanced performance and ultimately winning the race.

In our sales scenario here, the sports cap lid on its own is irrelevant; you must make clear to the customer the connection with the end result, i.e. the benefit that the sports cap lid brings to them, or the return on their investment.

Now before moving on, take time to consider carefully the real benefits of your product or service to the audience(s) you have chosen to target (the benefits may be different for different audiences).

Download and use the template *Exploring Pain & Gain – worksheet 2* to help you consider gains and pains for your target audience.

**www.winningsales.co.uk/resources**
···→ Exploring Pain & Gain worksheets 1 and 2

# How different are you – what are the alternatives?

When describing your product, be clear about what or whom you are up against because you need to position yourself against this backdrop. If you don't know, find out, either before your initial contact or meeting (research) or during your telephone call or meeting (via effective questioning). Essentially you need to find out what options or alternatives your customer has:

- Could they buy a competitive product? That is, a better or cheaper or more well-known option?

- Could they use an alternative solution? That is, do whatever they're trying to do in a different way without the fear or risk of introducing a new supplier.

- Is doing nothing at all or staying put a viable option? ("Life is just fine as it is.")

Why are you **clearly** the best and most logical option? You can only position yourself as the most obvious choice if you are aware of and can explore the above. Therefore put some time into researching your competitors and know how you stack up. Then prepare how you are going to clearly communicate your USPs to your potential customer.

**Your uniqueness – your USP (unique selling point)**

What makes you stand out from the crowd?

What is different, special or exciting about you, your product or your service?

Why should someone buy from you rather than from someone else?

## What's in it for them? What's your real value?

The bottom line in any purchase decision is 'what's in it for me' (often referred to as tuning into your buyer's WIIFM wavelength). Whilst some purchase decisions are more impulse buys and heart-led, in challenging market conditions more and more commitments to buy are logical purchase decisions with real consideration of Return on Investment (ROI).

The more clearly you can communicate ROI and the more significant the impact of this is, the easier you will make it for the buyer to make the decision to purchase, especially in high-value business-to-business sales. In the previous example of drinks bottles, sports cap lids and stained T-shirts, the real value or ROI is how much time (in the race) and money (on cleaning stained T-shirts) you save the customer, minus the cost of them investing in you. Always think how tangible this financial element is and whether you can quantify it in real terms. If you can prove it with evidence, backed up with case studies or testimonials, then so much the better!

---

**Example**

You sell a service which costs £6,000 (one-off cost).

By using your service, the company will save approximately £1,000 per month (you can demonstrate this, based on testimonials, case studies and research).

Therefore the potential cost savings in year one are £12,000.

$$\text{ROI} = \frac{£12,000 \text{ (saving)} - £6,000 \text{ (cost)}}{£6,000 \text{ (investment)}} \times 100\% = 100\% \text{ (Yr 1)}$$

So a virtual no-brainer! A 100% return on investment after one year, or a net saving of £6,000. Now you can consider the longer-term benefits, once the initial investment cost has been recovered!

---

It's important when trying to quantify your complete value and ROI that you truly think about the big picture and also consider intangible or less obvious, but still critical, gains. It's worth trying to explore and quantify these gains with your buyer, e.g. happier staff, less product returns, less time spent on complaints or happier customers, more positive word-of-mouth, referrals and repeat business. What's this worth to the business and what's this worth to the buyer? The more you can quantify the benefit and value of your product or service, the less vague the sales dialogue will be and the more it becomes a logical outcome that a purchase will be made – it simply makes sense!

# 5

# Connecting

At this stage in our journey together, you will have gained clarity about:

- who specifically you wish to target
- the potential value to them of your product or service.

Your next step is to make the connection with the potential buyer. So what's the best way to do this – by phone, email, letter, formal introduction, networking event, LinkedIn?

First, let's be clear that there isn't one single best way to connect with your customer. It truly is a case of 'different strokes for different folks', both from your own perspective and from the potential buyer's point of view. What will work well in one situation for one buyer and seller, may fail miserably in another situation, even with the same seller and a different buyer, or a different buyer with the same seller. The key thing is to experiment and test different approaches. This way you'll discover which option delivers the best return on your time invested in selling.

## Tip: Don't get stuck in a rut

Avoid sticking to just one approach to selling or developing just one safe habit. Be brave, be bold and step outside your comfort zone. If you stick to what you've always done, you''ll end up always getting what you've always got. Maybe this has worked in the past, but maybe you're now missing significant opportunities only accessible via a different route. Times are changing and dramatically so; you will need to change and adapt too. Don't eliminate any possibility until you've tried it, and even then try, try, and try again.

# The rules of engagement

Regardless of how you choose to connect, there are some fundamental rules of engagement to observe.

1 Just do it! It's not about being perfect, it's about being proactive and gradually getting better as you go along.

2 Do it regularly, not in an ad hoc way. Making connections should become an ongoing, lifetime habit for successful selling and sustainable business growth. Every situation you find yourself in could potentially lead to a new connection – you just need to switch on your sales radar, whether that's at the bus stop, on the golf course or indeed in the doctor's waiting room!

3 Think 'little and often' when it comes to proactive business development, rather than seeing it as a formidable 'big mountain to climb'. Don't wait to put a day aside for making connections – it won't happen. It's more realistic to invest small and focused chunks of time instead.

4 Put connecting or 'prospecting' time in your diary (real or virtual) in red, and commit to it – or it may not happen. (If it's not the thing you most love doing, you will procrastinate and easily get distracted.) Develop a habit of setting a daily, weekly or monthly goal to make a certain number of new connections.

5 Always focus on your connection – your potential customer – and their need. Make it personal to them, not about 'prospect number x' on your list, otherwise you will come across as impersonal, scripted and false.

6 Adopt a simple system to manage your connections, otherwise you risk wasting time and effort (we explore this further in chapter 8, step 10).

7 Celebrate every yes and accept every no because every no gets you one step closer to a yes. Also remember, no today is not necessarily a no tomorrow. (We deal later with handling no and turning no into yes.)

8 Clarity, relevance and tenacity are key. Know who you need to speak to, what you're going to say, why your product or service will bring benefit to them and how you're going to convince them of this – and stick at it. Seek to gain agreement about staying in touch – how, when and how often.

9 Avoid becoming a stalker by varying your methods of engagement and timing appropriately. Seek to be spontaneous, relevant and interesting and not predictable, irrelevant and boring.

10 Remember that not everyone out there needs you now but someone does...soon. Spread the word clearly, in a focused way and repeat it; ultimately you will be heard.

# Warm prospects and cold prospects

A major consideration in relation to connecting, is whether to choose the warm or the cold route. Have you got warm leads, where you have a previous history with the person or have been, or could be, introduced by someone else? Or are you starting completely from scratch and have no option other than picking up the phone and calling cold?

## Warm prospects

The easiest option for many business people, and often the quickest way in, is to carefully examine your existing network of contacts. Who do you know from your entire past life (family, friends, college buddies, business associates, ex-colleagues...) who may be a potential customer or a promoter or introducer for your product or service?

---

**Working your network**

- Remember 'Shy bairns get nowt!' – roughly translated *(from Geordie, NE UK)* as 'If you don't ask you won't get!'

- Assume nothing! Don't make the mistake of assuming people know you're looking for or are interested in connections or business. It may be obvious to you, but you need to prompt people. Let them know you'd appreciate their introduction, connections, referrals, etc. Also don't assume they know what you do or what you do **now**. Educate them about 'the new you' – your products and services, the value of them, the benefit they offer, and who precisely your product or service can help.

---

## Cold prospects

Once you have exhausted your easy and obvious networks, you need to think of the big picture and be more strategic in your approach. There's a world full of people out there; think about who you'd *really* like to connect with rather than who it's *easiest* to connect with.

## Tip: Seek to aim high for maximum rewards

The most easily won business may not be the right long-term business although it's probably fine to help get you started. Be careful about filling your time and using your resources bagging the low-hanging, low value fruit. Not all business is good business. You may need to get the ladder out to climb the tree and pick the best of the crop right at the highest branch. It might not be easy, but it might be the most rewarding in the long term. Also the higher you reach, the less competition you'll meet – they didn't have your courage and stamina.

This is where many new businesses come unstuck: once they have exhausted the easy, or warm options, there is a reluctance to advance up the ladder into cold territory! You may never need to actually cold-call, but moving beyond the comfort and warmth of easily won, or known, connections may be the only way to reach a very specific person in an organisation. Only then can you be confident that you have truly connected with the decision-maker and your message has been heard and understood.

Let's briefly explore a range of options for connecting with strangers:

### Referrals

As already discussed above, this is really about maximising on every connection – personal and business – throughout your sales journey and business life. Always seek to give and get referrals as this is a two-way process. It's also true that the more referrals you give, the more referrals you'll receive. Be clear on what kind of referrals you seek and let people know.

The best time to ask for referrals is when you've done a good job, so don't be shy. Once someone knows, likes and trusts you, they will be happy to recommend you, but don't leave this to chance – ask. Also, even though people are unable to give you business themselves (due to budget, timescales, lack of authority, other commitments and obligations, etc.) – they may still like you and want to give you something else instead. So don't forget to ask that vital question: "Who else do you know who could benefit from this product or service?" or "Who else might be facing similar problems or have similar challenges or issues...?"

## Networking

We have touched on networking for referrals amongst your existing network. Now look beyond these comfort zones and seek to build other networks, either formal or informal. Explore the networking events or organisations in your area, or beyond, that are relevant to you and where you are likely to connect with your prospects or introducers. Try them out and decide which ones are for you. Not all will be relevant, so be discerning and don't waste your time.

## Tips: Networking

**1** Avoid wasting time at events which don't attract your specific **M·A·I·N** players.

**2** Avoid going to the same events over and over again and getting cosy. Suddenly you'll find you're no longer networking but meeting the same people and having nice chats and coffee – with zero outcome.

**3** Maximise on every networking event by proper advance planning and tenacious follow-up. Stay in touch with relevant prospects and opportunities or else you've wasted your time and money going in the first place.

## Speaking at events

Can you get yourself speaking at the front of the room, instead of listening at the back? Could you promote yourself effectively by speaking at events, as the expert? Search out local, regional and national opportunities and seek to raise your profile. If this appears daunting, perhaps you could team up with someone or find easier, more friendly groups initially.

## Membership

Think about the kind of networks you are trying to build. You want networks which will add value to you. Are there professional organisations, business clubs, charity boards, guilds or institutes which you could join either as a member or even on the board? Think first about what you can offer of value and give generously; then think about what you might hope to gain. The outcome might simply be confidence-building, or an improved feel good factor, or may be more tangible, such as new connections, increased credibility or heightened kudos.

## You as the expert

How can you position yourself as the expert in your field and so bring exposure through articles and media coverage? Can you write articles, contribute to newspapers, blogs, etc.? Can you promote yourself effectively to your general target audience and then maximise your effort by sending these contributions to your specific prospect list with a note saying 'Thought this might be of interest', or 'This may help in relation to what we discussed'? It's a great way of warming up prospects or keeping warm prospects from going cold. Have you a story to tell about you and your business, and can you get the press, radio or even TV excited and interested in you and help you warm up your connections? Exposure through public relations is very often free!

## Social media

This highly topical, rapidly evolving marketing strategy offers myriad possibilities for connecting and staying in touch with opportunities, prospects, influencers and promoters. If used effectively (and not abused), the opportunities are truly endless in terms of developing and promoting your own profile as well as learning about and connecting with others in your extended network. Invest time in understanding the latest rules of engagement whether this is with LinkedIn, Twitter, blogging, Facebook, etc. The rules of engaging in this way are clearly new, and some of these rules challenge the more traditional sales and marketing techniques or norms, so invest time and energy exploring how these can best work for you.

## Email or letter

You may choose to introduce yourself formally by letter or, less formally, by email. The key thing with either is to follow up. Never send a letter or email introduction and then sit back and wait for the phone to ring; it may, but it probably won't. The reason(s) you haven't had a reply is not necessarily that someone isn't interested, but rather:

- they haven't actually received or read your communication
- they haven't understood what you do and the benefits that this will bring them
- they *are* interested – but not now
- they *are* interested – but haven't prioritised the time to get back in touch with you.

Remember it's a busy, cluttered marketplace, so buyers are forced to filter out unnecessary, unimportant noise. It's vital to follow up on all your communication to truly connect and get real answers. In fact, it is vital to follow up on everything in sales – full stop! Nothing should be left to chance, to luck, or to your potential buyer's time management skills. Take the lead and keep control.

## Tip: Communication

Don't over-rely on email as an easy way of communicating with a stranger and as a means of avoiding picking up the phone. Email has its place, but it is one-way communication and can be relatively cold. It's also easier to ignore or reject the written word than the spoken word. So before you start tapping on the keyboard, think whether it might make more sense to pick up the phone.

### Telephone

The question I am often asked in relation to connecting via the telephone is: "Do you just pick up the phone or do you try to warm the prospect up first by sending a letter or email?"

Personally I am a big fan of initially just picking up the phone for a 'chat', for the following reasons:

1   I believe most things you send through get deleted (in the case of email) or end up in the bin (in the case of snail-mail post) or get filtered out by

personal assistants or other gatekeepers, so you are generally wasting time or money or both.

2   It makes more sense to send something through *after* you've spoken, once you've connected (physically and mentally) and understood the prospect. Whatever you now send, especially if you've tailored it (following your chat), will be far more specific, relevant and memorable.

3   Following up on something you've just sent can mean having to overcome the initial pre-conceived barriers or foregone conclusions of your buyer or their gatekeeper. Or actually they've already decided not to take your call.

Successful telephone connecting is all about having a positive mind-set. Don't get hung up on the fact that others do it badly (the aggressive, rude, obnoxious 'semi-professional' cold-callers). Decide to be different – mentally remove the word and image of cold-calling and start thinking about having meaningful telephone conversations with people you can help... if you can't help or they don't wish to engage, that's fine! You have already established in your mind clarity around your value – what you do offers serious value to people. Now you are simply ringing up to share this opportunity with others. You are not trying to sell anything, you are purely seeking to engage, explore and see if you can help.

Don't focus on "What will I say?" and having the perfect script; think instead about "What will I ask?" How can you have a meaningful chat with someone about their problems, issues and needs in relation to your area of expertise? (We will explore your questioning technique in some detail in chapter 7 in terms of the meeting and this will apply just as much in the telephone 'meeting'.)

You may find a value in experimenting with 'your story' as your hook or way-in, but remember to keep it short (30 seconds maximum)! If you are the managing director of a new company and have developed a new product or service in response to a market challenge you identified, then share this personal and relevant pain with your prospect. Seek to explore: Has your prospect had similar experiences in the past or are they likely to have in the future and, therefore, be interested in a dialogue and possibly a 'fix'? What do you do that's better, faster or more effective than everything else out there and why do you think this may be of interest to your prospect?

For a good telephone sales conversation, focus on the following key points:

- **your potential customer**: the person, the human being (not the number on your list, or their job title); have a clear positive mental image of the individual, their role and the challenges they're facing

- **your hook or opening**: keep it brief (30 seconds maximum), clear and interesting
- **the questions you will ask**: how will you engage and ensure a two-way dialogue and not a one-way monologue
- **the value you offer and can prove**: why should they bother talking to you, meeting with you, testing your product, or buying your service
- **your desired outcome**: your 'close' – the arrangement of a meeting, a trial, or a purchase (and a fall-back plan)
- **your tone**: be passionate, but slow, clear, sincere and in charge! Don't rush or be apologetic
- **what if…**: be prepared for objections, challenges, questions and, of course, a no!

## And finally – The 7 to 11 Rule

Once you start thinking about connecting, it's vital to be aware of The 7 to 11 Rule. Market research shows that it can take from seven and eleven connections before a customer 'gets' the message and acts. There are some significant pointers to take from this:

1   Don't give up too soon! Many people pull back just before the buyer was about to say yes. Stick at it: tenacity is everything.

2   No today does not mean no tomorrow. It's all about timing, clarity, need, budget and sometimes even luck!

3   Having a system and methodology is vital if you are going to manage this reconnection process successfully.

4   Multiple and varied methods of connecting work best. A mixture of phone, email, personal contact, and 'bumping into' works best, and means you are approaching different people in different ways.

5   Vary the time when you try to connect – you will have highs and lows during your day and your prospect will too. Tune in to the most optimal time of day to connect with your type of decision-maker; given their predictable work patterns, when are they most likely to be available and not available?

6   What works best for one buyer–seller combo may not be right for another, so experiment. Dare to be different!

# Part Two

---

# Sales Meeting Success (Your PDP Strategy)

Arising from your success at connecting, you have now secured that highly prized outcome: your first meeting. Please remember that you get only one shot at creating a great first impression and getting your potential buyer onside and interested. It may take a number of further meetings to seal the deal but the opportunity to do this will depend on how well prepared you are for this vital first meeting and then what you do next.

 *You never get a second chance to make a first impression.*

# 12 common sales meeting mistakes

1 Not being prepared – doing it 'on a wing and a prayer'!

2 Too much or too little rapport-building – turn off, not on.

3 Too much talking – not enough listening.

4 Dumping rather than matching – 'The Vomit Sell'.

5 Not involving the prospect – it's about them and their pain, not about you.

6 Not clarifying the decision-making group – the **M·A·I·N** players.

7 Not clarifying budget and timescales.

8 Missing buying signals.

9 Not picking up on objections or not removing barriers to the sale.

10 Not closing tightly or not closing at all – leaving too many loose ends.

11 Poor follow-up or loss of control.

12 Not maximising every opportunity – not switching on to other opportunities (LTV).

# Your PDP strategy (pre–during–post meeting)

Your sales success will be greatly enhanced by adopting what I term a PDP strategy to every sales activity you undertake, whether this is a sales meeting, a networking event, a sales telephone call, a letter or a proposal. Stop and think of the three distinct phases – Pre, During and Post – to ensure maximum return. Don't just show up and hope for the best!

In this book I'll focus on applying the Pre–During–Post strategy to the initial sales meeting, but it should be easy to see how the same approach will be useful with *any* sales activity:

**Pre**     What do I do before I go to the meeting to be best prepared and positioned to succeed?

**During**     What do I do during the meeting to get the best possible outcome for today and to pave the way for future success?

**Post**     What do I do after the meeting to ensure optimum results and maximum return on the time I've invested?

By applying this structured approach to each and every sales initiative, you'll guarantee yourself significantly enhanced sales outcomes. Focus on your *input* (what you *can* control) to ensure the best chance of the most favourable *output* (what you *can't* control). Too often in business I see poor return on sales activity due to poor planning and poor objective setting, a lack of structure to the activity itself and an equally disappointing or lack-lustre follow-up.

Think of all the email requests or telephone enquiries you've made when you've been weighing up whether to buy something – and how few suppliers have actually followed up. Consequently your initial interest waned or just got buried on your desk and forgotten. You never bought, or took action, and the seller never even knew why!

Now, let's break this strategic Pre-During–Post approach down further into *The 12 Winning Steps of Logical Conclusion Selling*© to ensure optimal results.

# The 12 Winning Steps of Logical Conclusion Selling©

**Maximise the opportunity**

Exploring Lifetime Value (LTV) of opportunities; an introduction to cross-selling, upselling, referrals and repeat business.

**Review performance and celebrate**

What worked? and what didn't? what can be improved for next time? Celebrate your success and that of others.

**Follow up**

The vital importance of taking control and doing what you said you would do; managing your prospects and sales pipeline.

**Gain commitment**

Close; agreeing firmly what happens next – the sale or the next meeting or the next connection.

**Explore and handle objections**

Are there any barriers to moving forward (price, risk, another supplier or other decision-makers)? Separate the real objections from the fob-offs or diversions.

**Match your solution and create value**

Clearly demonstrate how your product or service fits the agreed needs and delivers real Return on Investment.

**Summarise and agree need**

Getting on the same wavelength; first buying signals.

During-meeting phase

**Explore and understand your prospect and their needs**

Avoid dumping and begin fact-finding – the vital importance of questioning and listening; ExtraExtra©.

**Set the scene**

Vital first impressions, agreeing agenda and mutual objectives – your opening hook or positioning statement.

**Get there professionally** 3

Plan your journey and arrival. What do you need in order to be best prepared?

2

**Research the opportunity**

What do you know? What do you need to find out? What assumptions can you make?

Pre-meeting phase

**Set your objectives** 1

Define your meeting objectives. Aim high and think of the big picture.

61

# 6

# The Pre-meeting Phase

Preparing for your sales meeting comprises three steps:

step 1:    set your objectives

step 2:    research the opportunity

step 3:    get there professionally.


## Step 1    Set your objectives

You can only determine the success of your meeting and evaluate progress if, from the outset, you were clear on your objectives. The clearer and more focused you are on what you hope to achieve, the more likely you are to achieve it. If you're just going along for 'a bit of a chat', then that's all you may end up having. However, if you're going along with the clear objective of coming away with a specific result, then you are more likely to achieve this. It's all about having a purpose and being in control. This is not about being pushy or forceful – it's simply giving focus and direction to everything you do. It's your meeting – manage it and don't leave the outcome to chance.

### Possible objectives for the sales meeting

- Get the sale or the business or 'do the deal' (in a one-stage sales meeting).

- Get to the next step – agree the next meeting or follow-up action (in a two-stage sales meeting).

- Explore, understand and agree your client's needs; identify gaps and opportunities.

- Explore the decision-making hierarchy and internal buying process.

- Explore other opportunities – Who else? Where else? What else?

- Build a relationship and brand for future sales situations; be memorable.

- Gather market intelligence regarding your product and your competition.

## Tips: Setting objectives

**1** Make sure you are setting your objectives high enough, with the ultimate prize in mind. Do not set your sights too low or that is all you will get. Think about the big picture. If you have a product or service where it is possible to close in one meeting, do not feel you need to drag things out to a second meeting. Don't procrastinate and waste time. Be confident without being pushy!

**2** Yes is the real prize but no is acceptable too! Seek clarity above all else and avoid having a bulging pipeline of 'maybe's', which are not real opportunities. Be honest with yourself and understand when 'maybe' or 'leave it with me' does actually mean no!

## Step 2     Research the opportunity

Once clear on your objectives, think about what else you need to know or find out prior to the meeting in order to achieve your objectives. Invest appropriate time in some pre-meeting research. The amount of time and resource you invest should be in proportion to the value of the opportunity or potential opportunity. It doesn't do to spend days on research if your potential sale is worth only a couple of quid! Equally if you are selling a high-value item for a few million pounds, a couple of weeks' research might be appropriate. However avoid using research as a delaying tactic – get moving!

The purpose of good research is to help plan and therefore help ensure your meeting goes well, specifically your questioning phase and objection handling. It will help you decide what gaps you will need to fill in during step 5 (exploration phase) and will also arm you for step 8 (handling objections).

You should acquire basic information (size of company, number of staff, turnover, etc.) from the internet, Companies House, etc., and not waste valuable meeting time asking trite questions to which answers are readily and publicly accessible (as you won't appear very professional). The more you know, the more empowered you will feel and the more confidence you will instil in your prospect. Your potential customer will feel valued that you have done your homework and can focus and structure the meeting accordingly.

Your research should be on two levels:

### Macro, or company, level

- **Size of company** – turnover, profitability, number of employees, other relevant financial information.

- **Ownership and decision-making powers** – where else, who else, how does it all fit; decide your point of entry.

- **Type of products and services used** – relative to your offering.

- **History, politics, current affairs in relation to their business** – what's hot, what's not; any media tit-bits of relevance.

- **The company's ambitions, plans and strategic direction.**

- **The client's other options** – who else do they buy from or what else do they do or could they do, instead of doing business with you?

- **Anything else** – specific to your product, service or business.

### Micro, or personal, level (with the decision-maker – M·A·I·N players)

In our very open, social media-driven society, many people have very public profiles as a result of LinkedIn, Facebook, Twitter, etc. and you can find out a wealth of information by searching for a person on Google. Read about them on their own website, if they have one. You are looking to understand:

- **The responsibility structure and their decision-making power** – who reports to whom?

- **Personal stuff** – family, affiliations, interests, awards, recognitions.

- **Their track record** – past employment, past or current involvement in boards, charities or organisations.

- **Common connections or interests.**

Download and use the template **Opportunity Factfile** to give yourself a structure for this process. You may also find it useful to refer back to chapter 3 at this point.

**www.winningsales.co.uk/resources**
⋯→ Opportunity Factfile template

## Step 3    Get there professionally

This is about the tools and preparation you need to consider in order to ensure you physically arrive as a competent professional. It includes:

- **Journey planning** – the route, car park location, loose change for car parking fees.

- **Having the correct address** – with postcode and telephone number (to call should you be unavoidably delayed).

- **Samples, brochures, business cards** – neat, tidy and clean.

- **A formal presentation** – if required; avoid 'dumping' a presentation on people or simply handing it over.

- **Price lists** - again, if required. But do avoid simply handing over price lists as if you're embarrassed about them. Instead discuss them, explain them and demonstrate value and Return on Investment.

- **Pens, calculator, colour swatches, notepad** – anything else specific to your business.

- **A clean and tidy car** – it will be visible in the car park and reflects on you. You may even end up having to give someone a lift and they won't be impressed by a mountain of sweet wrappers, CDs or children's toys.

- **Your appearance** – physically fit for purpose. Think of the person or people you are meeting and dress appropriately. What impression are you trying to create and does your dress and appearance reflect that? You will be judged on a first impression, so take care; you may not be allowed to prove yourself beyond your appearance!

- **Your attitude** – mentally fit for purpose. Are you thinking positively and confidently about your value and purpose? Have you parked any negative thoughts, fears and concerns? Are you ready for a successful meeting? Is this reflected in your body language as you walk through the door? Check your posture, make and maintain eye contact, watch what you do with your hands, and what facial expression you wear.

### Tips: Getting there professionally

**1** Always ring ahead if you're running late – don't just show up late and apologise. Most people are sympathetic to unforeseeable events, but do build in some buffer for traffic delays, finding a parking spot, etc.

**2** Always confirm the address of the meeting venue and postcode and ask about parking options – don't assume the address on a website is the right one; offices and people move and websites aren't always up to date.

**3** Dress up or down depending on the atmosphere you're trying to create but always remain professional and feel confident. Avoid being too slick or looking like the stereotypical sales person, especially if this is not appropriate for the sector.

# 7

# The During-meeting Phase

The 'During' phase is all about leading your prospect on an exciting journey, with a beginning, a middle and an end – the end being the ultimate decision to buy from you or work with you. This 'end' or result should be a logical conclusion, not forced or coerced.

I cannot emphasise enough the importance of having an underlying structure to your meeting rather than simply winging it. If you don't have a structure in place, certainly in your early days of selling, you run the risk of being at sixes and sevens, losing control and even forgetting why you are there in the first place. Consequently you risk leaving empty-handed or with empty promises and then struggling to reconnect.

The 'During' phase consists of six simple and logical steps:

step 4:     setting the scene

step 5:     understanding your prospect and their needs

step 6:     summarising and agreeing needs and benefits

step 7:     matching your solution to needs and creating value

step 8:     exploring and handling concerns or objections

step 9:     closing and gaining commitment or getting a yes!

It is impossible to leapfrog to step 9 and get a yes without working your way through steps 4 to 8. Often, when I see or hear people struggling to close their sales, it is because they've missed out on one of the above critical steps. You cannot close what is not closable! If the proposed solution doesn't fit the buyer's needs, the buyer won't be buying, or if they do, they will forever associate you with selling them something which didn't suit or wasn't needed and they won't come back. Worse still, the disgruntled buyer will talk badly about you forever.

It's also important to note that along this journey through steps 4 to 9 you are gathering mini-yes's. If you do this successfully, you will end up with one big yes as a final outcome or close. If you meet with disagreement or dissonance at any one step, and don't bottom this before you move on, you'll get stuck at step 9 and be unable to close.

You can only close when you are hearing or sensing yes all the way.

**Which mini-yes's might you collect along the way?**

Step 4    You both agree the purpose of the meeting and a
          final desired outcome ... yes

Step 5    You and the prospect both understand the current
          situation and the key needs ... yes

Step 6    You both understand the main needs and the
          'significant gain' in fixing 'the pain' ... yes

Step 7    Your product fixes the agreed pain, achieves the
          desired 'gain' and represents value or Return on
          Investment ... yes

Step 8    Any issues blocking the sale are overcome or agreed
          not to be relevant ... yes

Step 9    Let's move forward; buy or make a commitment to
          the next step ... YES!

Alternatively, if at any stage during steps 4 to 9 you are hearing, feeling or observing no or reluctance, don't push on! Stop and check what is happening. You cannot push your way to the end of the sale or you will meet resistance when you try to close. Lead your prospect on this journey and understand their concerns and challenges along the way. Never carry on regardless; the prospect has to be on board all the way. Poor sales people try to push the sale through; effective, successful sales people lead the buyer towards a purchase or logical outcome.

## Step 4    Set the scene

Keep it simple and focus on three main objectives when you first meet your prospect:

1   Build rapport, credibility and trust.

2   Get onto the same wavelength and agree the purpose of the meeting.

3   Get attention and interest.

### Building rapport, credibility and trust

Your first objective is to be at ease, both physically and mentally, and thereby put your potential customer at ease too.

**Mentally:** In your mind, see your buyer as a normal person, just like you, regardless of how they come across. We are all different but essentially equal – they may have a bigger house, faster car, more or less kids, different or the same hobbies and interests, but when it comes down to it, we are all human beings in that we were born, will live, perhaps multiply and die. Don't let yourself be put off by thinking that someone is more, or less, important than you – they're not. If you have researched well, then you have a real value and purpose for being in this place and having this meeting. See yourself and your buyer as collaborators rather than adversaries.

**Physically:** Believing that you and your potential buyer are equal and that you have real value to offer will impact subconsciously on your physical appearance. You need to reflect this in positive and confident body language:

- use a firm handshake

- keep good eye contact

- adopt an open and relaxed posture

- don't fidget.

Don't forget that the first impression counts and most people make their mind up within the first 30 seconds of meeting you.

75

**55% of the first impression in a sales meeting is created by body language; 38% by your tone of voice and only 7% by your words or what you say.**

As you progress through the meeting and your relationship develops over time, you should be building likeability, credibility and trust. Ideally, try to find common ground and have a bit of an initial chat (or make some small talk), but don't be false or insincere. Chat about your positive observations in the car park, lobby, etc., or mention something you've noticed on the wall, something you've picked up in the newspaper, on their website, or on LinkedIn. From your research you might be aware that you have something in common – a mutual friend, shared hobby or membership of the same body?

A word of caution though: Not everyone wants a chat, so read the signals carefully. If someone is being abrupt, it doesn't necessarily mean they are being rude or uninterested, they may simply want you to get on with it. So adapt this rapport-building phase to suit your buyer and don't overdo it. Don't force idle or unnecessary chit-chat.

### Agreeing purpose – getting on the same wavelength

This is your opportunity to take control of the meeting and move from light banter to structure and purpose. This is where you suggest the meeting purpose and agenda and get your first yes!

> "So, Tom, thanks for inviting me along – it's great to have the opportunity of finally meeting you. The purpose of today is to get a deeper understanding of your business and needs, specifically in relation to X [the problem areas you are hoping to resolve]. Then I'd like to share some ideas with you on how I feel we can help and add value, get your feedback and agree a way forward. Is that okay with you?"
> ... "Yes!"

It might also be useful to agree how much time they have available so that you can tailor your approach accordingly.

Essentially you are setting and agreeing an agenda as follows:

- **explore** their need – focus on the buyer
- **match** their need – focus on the solution
- **close** – focus on a collaborative way forward.

This format will:

a) allow you to set up and agree a meeting structure which follows steps 5 to 9 of the 12 steps already outlined

b) stop you going into 'vomit mode' and just dumping irrelevant, or too much information on your prospect; in other words, it allows you to tailor your pitch to the customer's specific needs

c) get agreement from the buyer that, subject to your solution matching their need, you can do business; in other words, you are agreeing from the start that the purpose of the meeting is to close and that this is legitimate, acceptable and in the best interest of both parties ("As we agreed at the start...!")

d) bring to the surface straight away any barriers to closing, for example, "Well, actually I will need to involve someone else before I can move this forward...,' or "We are meeting someone else tomorrow..." or "We are not planning to do anything right now, we're just exploring options ..." – and that is acceptable, too. It's best to discover these things at the outset and deal with them, lest they surface at the end and block your sale.

### Grabbing attention and interest – turning them on, not off!

When setting the scene, you may need a brief, but attention-grabbing, introduction on what you do and who you are (make it a maximum of two minutes). This is not always necessary and sometimes you can go straight in at step 5. This is my preferred route, based on the principle that the less said initially the better, as this gives you more freedom later to adapt your pitch. However, for people new to sales, I suggest you prepare for the question "So what exactly do you do" or "Tell me a little about yourself'. The clue here is 'a little', not 'a lot'! Don't fall into the trap of giving a long and boring pitch at the start, which will not be tailored and may not be relevant to your specific customer. The only result this would have is to kill any interest that might have been starting to grow.

Some thoughts on what you may wish to include in your introduction:

- **Your track record** – specific to this person and their industry sector. Avoid trying to be all things to all people. For example, don't say, "We sell to everyone, large and small and do everything from a–z"; instead, be specific and tailored: "We have a well-established track record dealing with companies similar to yours in the X sector (unless there's a competitive element!)", or "Other HR managers are finding significant gain in using our service to improve…". As a general rule, if you're speaking to HR managers, share how you help HR managers with their problems; if you're speaking to chemical engineers, talk about how you have helped chemical engineers with their challenges, etc.

- **Your value and return on investment** – briefly describe what you do and how it makes an impact. Mention tangible wins, for example in terms of percentage increases, pounds saved, number of customers gained, days saved, etc.

- **Your USP** – explain what makes you different, special and better than everyone else or the alternative options.

This is your positioning statement and should set the scene for what follows. The aim is not to tell everything straight away but to grab the buyer's attention, leave them keen to find out more, and create a situation which will allow you to now move to step 5.

Get comfortable with this opening pitch and it will serve you well for all initial sales connection points including your telephone introduction, your networking events, the start of a formal presentation and your mailshots. Be able to communicate clearly and succinctly what you do and what the potential gains are for the specific audience. Will your buyer sit up and listen or think "Oh no, here we go!"?

# Step 5 — Explore and understand your prospect and their needs

Having opened your meeting successfully and set the scene, you will now move into exploration mode. Your specific purpose is to explore what your prospect is currently doing, how it's working for them, what problems they might be having, what solutions they are looking for (if they know) and, ultimately, how best you can help them.

In order to explore need effectively it is useful at this point to understand *open* and *closed* questions and to be clear about when to use each of them during a sales meeting.

| **?** ■ Open questions | **?** ■ Closed questions |
|---|---|
| **Who?, Where?, Why?, What?, When?, How?** | **Any question which results in a yes/no answer, for example, "Is that correct?"** |
| *Useful for: opening, exploring, gathering information, building rapport, showing interest, stopping yourself talking and getting others to talk.* | *Useful for: getting agreement, confirmation, clarity and closure.* |

The simple method I have developed for an effective questioning technique is called ExtraExtra©. It combines the use of open and closed questions.

In chapter 4 we talked about moving your prospect from place A to place B – a better place, with you. You can only take them to a better place by helping them understand place A 'today' (not so great) and by helping them explore the possibilities of place B 'tomorrow' (so much better!). Then you can clearly reflect and agree that place B *is* better than place A, and significantly so! The Winning Sales ExtraExtra Formula© will allow you to explore this effectively.

On the following pages is an example of how ExtraExtra© might work.

# ExtraExtra© Phase 1

 plore  oday

**Place A**

Start this process by asking the prospect questions which explore what they are currently doing now (today), how this is working, what the impact is, the gains from doing it this way, and the pains.

Some sample questions:

*"What are you currently doing when it comes to X?"* (being your area of expertise, best expressed as a problem)

*For example, if you provide search engine optimisation solutions, ask: "What do you currently do to ensure people find your website if they're looking for your type of product?"*

*"How is this working for you? What do you like? What do you not like about it?"*

*"What have you tried in the past? How has that worked?"*

*"Who uses (manages) this? What's the impact of this on their life, their work or their business?"*

*"What does Y think (Y being the boss, customers or the staff)?"*

*"What challenges are you currently facing? What's the biggest pain?"*

Once you feel you've understood the 'today' situation, reflect this back to the prospect to ensure you've understood everything correctly and not missed anything.

 eflect

*"So, Tom, can I just summarise what I've understood about your current situation?"*

Reiterate the main issues you have identified – and where you can help.

*Pain 1 – "I understand the main challenges you are facing are..."*

*Pain 2 – "The impact of this on the business is..."*

*Pain 3 – "The key people affected are..."*

**A** gree

Now seek agreement and a yes!

*"Is that correct? "*

... *"Yes!"* or *"Well actually, I didn't quite mean that..."*

*"Anything missing?"*

– *"Yes, I forgot to mention..."* or *"No, that's spot on."*

# ExtraExtra© Phase 2

 plore  omorrow

Now advance this process by exploring the future (tomorrow). What are the needs, expectations, hopes, dreams, challenges and rewards?

Some sample questions:

*"What would you like to achieve in the future?"*

*"What would be the impact of that?"*

*"On whom?' 'Anyone else?"*

*"Can you quantify that?"*

*"How would that look, feel or be?" (visualise the solution)*

*"What challenges might you need to overcome in order to achieve your goal?"*

*"In an ideal world, what would you most like to achieve?"*

As before, reflect this back to check you've understood correctly and not missed anything – and to get another yes!

**R** eflect

*"So, Tom, I'd like to summarise what I've understood to be your main objectives and priorities going forward and the benefits of that to you/ your business/your staff/your customers"*

*Gain 1 – Removing or improving Pain 1 = Priority 1*

*Gain 2 – Removing or improving Pain 2 = Priority 2*

*Gain 3 – Removing or improving Pain 3 = Priority 3*

**A** gree

*"Is that correct?"* – Yes or no.

– "Yes, I forgot to mention..."    or    "No, that's spot on."

**Other important questions to ask**

- Who will be involved in the final decision on this? (during step 5 identify the decision-making person)

- Who else might have a say in this? (identify the decision-making group)

- What timescales are you considering? (identify the urgency)

- What sort of budget has been allocated? (identify the budget)

- Who or what else are you considering? (identify the competition or alternatives)

- Is there anything else I should be aware of? (identify objections or barriers to closing or moving forward)

At the end of step 5, you should be confident that:

- we (the seller and the buyer) both understand the current situation and the pros and cons of the status quo

- we both understand where the buyer would like to be, what the objectives are and what the benefits are in going there.

Now you're ready to move on.

## Tips: Effective sales questioning

**1** Ask and then listen – to what's said and also implied (don't rush on). Learn the art of intuitive listening – what is my prospect really saying? Probe if you're unclear.

**2** Be genuine in your interest – remember you are building rapport and likeability. We like people who are interested in and focused on us, our business and our lives.

**3** Use open questions to explore and to open up dialogue with people.

**4** Use closed questions to close, gain clarity, gain commitment, gain direction or to channel your questions.

**5** Use less sensitive, more open and general questions at the start of the session.

**6** Save the more personal, tricky questions until you have built some trust and credibility – but don't forget to ask them.

**7** Don't answer people's questions for them if they are struggling. Learn to zip your lips and allow them to find their own answers; don't make assumptions, lead or interrupt.

**8** Prepare your questions well. Don't think "What am I going to say?" at a sales meeting or on a telephone call; instead think "What am I going to ask?". Don't rely on chance; plan your critical questions in advance. What questions will give you the most valuable information?

**9** Don't ask silly questions – ones you should know the answers to already if you'd done your homework. Use the meeting to confirm that information is correct and up to date.

**10** And finally, remember the old saying 'you have two ears and one mouth – use them in that proportion'. Listen twice as much as you talk. After every meeting, reflect on who did the talking; if it was all you, then something was wrong!

 # Summarise and agree need

This half-way point is short but vital. It offers you and the buyer a chance to stop, pause, rewind and check that you are both on the same page – the customer's page. Remember that up to now you've not discussed your product or service in any great depth. Get step 6 right and you will find:

- it sets the scene perfectly for you to introduce a very tailored and precise presentation which perfectly matches the customer's specific need – step 7

- it cuts out or minimises objections or resistance ("Yes but!") – step 8

- it facilitates a very smooth Logical Conclusion© close – it simply makes sense to buy (a virtual no-brainer!) – step 9.

In other words, if the buyer is currently in place A – which you both have agreed is not great – and you can help take them to place B – which they have agreed would be significantly better – assuming the value of the benefits is significantly greater than the costs of going there – then it simply makes perfect sense to take action and buy!

So during step 6, you need to simply summarise everything you have discussed in step 5, and put your slant on it. Start laying the foundations for your pending recommendations and solutions.

*Seller: "So, Tom, before I share with you my ideas on how I believe I can help, I'd like to summarise where I feel we've now got to. I'd like to make sure I've got this right and I'm not missing anything. Is that okay?"*

*Buyer: "Yeah, sure!"* (another yes! – if no, find out what's wrong or missing)

*Seller: "Currently when it comes to problem X, you're solving it in the following way"* – you now outline place A – the current solution or alternative, or nothing!

*"What you like about this is...."* – you now outline some benefits of place A, knowing that you too can offer this.

*"What you're not so keen on is... because it's causing you the following problems"* – you now highlight the pain of place A and the real impact of that pain (on customers, profits, staff...) knowing you can fix it.

*"What you'd really like going forward is to be able to create the following vision (outline place B). The impact on the business or for you would be x, y and z."* (highlight significant gains or potential benefits).

*"If we were to quantify that, we're looking at a saving of £££s or a gain of £££s, as well as the more difficult-to-quantify benefits of g and h. Is that correct?"*

*Buyer:* "Yes!"

*Seller:* "Is there anything I've left out or we've forgotten that might be important before we move on?" (your chance to flush out any 'buts' at this stage before you present your solution)

*Buyer:* Either:

a) *"No – spot on, that pretty much sums everything up for now."* You can now move to step 7 – this is another yes!

or

b) *"Well actually..."* You now need to clarify, explore further, remove barriers and revisit the summary and get a yes, before moving on.

## Tips: Summarising and agreeing

Don't start presenting your product until you and the buyer are in agreement about the main issues and the merits of making a change, otherwise you will start talking, but the buyer has other issues going on in their head and isn't fully listening or open to your solution. It's far easier to preach to the almost-converted!

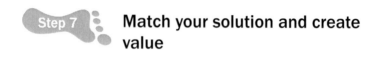

# Match your solution and create value

Some people would refer to this as the 'presentation phase'. However I hesitate to call it that because it implies:

- It's one-way.
- It's rehearsed and planned.
- It's not tailored to the audience.
- It's 'vomit-sell' – talk, talk, talk.

It also conjures up the image of the stereotypical sales rep arriving with their stereotypical black folder, which they then force the buyer to look through, or alternatively with their laptop and more techie, but equally boring, PowerPoint presentation.

I prefer to call this step the 'matching phase'. You are now going to match your product to the needs of your potential client. This is not a generic presentation, but a carefully mapped, two-way dialogue which links perfectly back to step 6 – otherwise that step was irrelevant!

There are two possibilities with the timing of step 7 – either do it now or come back another day. This will depend on the complexity of your product and whether you have to go away and pull information or prices together based on what you've just heard or whether you have the flexibility, knowledge and skills to do this now. You also need to consider whether the right people are in the room. If it makes sense and you are able to do so, then do it now; avoid procrastination and move forward confidently.

However, for others, a second meeting is essential in order to pull together the required information, prices, etc. and that is fine. I just caution you not to build in return visits when this is avoidable; you may not get back in!

It might be useful to refer back to chapter 4 before moving on.

You will have noticed that we are now at step 7 and up to now I have not suggested that you present your product or service to your customer. Have a think about this and consider why I am asking you to delay presenting until step 7. For many people new to sales, this is really hard – after all you've been asked to come and present!

Many novice sales people would have been straight in there, either with their presentation as step 1 or maybe step 2, after a bit of false chit-chat.

Hopefully you'll have followed me this far and understand that by waiting until step 7 to present, you are guaranteeing the following:

- a clear and tailored matching which is customer-focused, not vague or waffly
- your conversation demonstrates that you understand your customer and their vision
- your customer will see, hear and feel themselves in your conversation because you will talk in their language about their issues and concerns
- you are presenting price in terms of value, investment and ROI for them, rather than just a cost
- price can be broken down into manageable chunks, which relate to specific benefits
- your buyer can be led on a journey – their agreed journey – from where they are now, to where they want to be, and with you – it just makes sense.

If you choose to proceed with step 7 at your first meeting, here are some key pointers:

- be specific to the needs of the client and their industry sector, company size, corporate background, etc. by talking in their language, about their issues
- be specific to the needs you explored in step 5
- be relevant to the customer's priorities
- clearly demonstrate how you address the agreed pains identified and deliver the agreed gains required
- demonstrate the tangible and quantifiable gains as well as the intangible gains which are less easy to quantify
- explore price in relation to value of investment or ROI, based on the gains you've identified
- clearly position yourself against the competition or alternative options by stating your USPs

- include evidence of your claims with proof (your track record)
- outline the way forward as a simple and inevitable logical conclusion.

> **Summarise as follows:**
>
> **This is you now (place A) ... this is you and us together (place B) ... this is how we'll get there ... this is how it will look, feel, sound and be ... this will be the benefit ... this will be the cost ... it makes sense ... let's do it! ... Logical Conclusion Selling©.**

Sometimes you may not be able to complete this matching step in your first meeting because of the complexity of your offering and the additional information you will need to gather to present effectively. If you're adopting a two-meeting approach, then the purpose of the first meeting is fact-finding and meeting two will be a more detailed 'product mapping'. You may in fact need to bring back colleagues to do this with you, or indeed you may wish to invite colleagues from the client's company to participate in order to get the best ROI and win a buying decision from a number of people.

A few words of warning about adopting a two-meeting approach:

1   Be careful you don't build unnecessary sales steps into your process and prolong the sales journey. Sometimes people avoid matching at a first meeting because of insecurities and they develop a habit of always coming back another day. Check how far you can really take things in the first meeting; could you actually match and close, or at least make a provisional close subject to following up with some price information later? Find a balance between procrastinating and being too pushy.

2   Even if you have to come back another day, still go through a mini-version of steps 7, 8 and 9 at the first meeting. Do a mini-mapping session (step 7), highlighting your USPs, track record and demonstrating where you feel you will be able to add tangible value. *Make sure you have got them hooked* – really keen and interested enough to want you back, excited and wanting more. Seek some initial commitment. You will

also still need to flush out objections (step 8) and close effectively for the purpose of confirming a second meeting date (step 9).

# Explore and handle objections

When you have finished matching, you may either move directly to close (step 9) or if you're still not sure, you may want to use a trial close to check how you're doing or seek feedback:

*"So, Tom, based on this, what are your thoughts at this stage?"* (an open question which elicits general feedback to allow you to close more effectively);

*"So, Tom, is this the sort of solution you were looking for?"* (a good closed question to use if you're reasonably confident of getting a yes but just checking).

You will at this point either get a yes or sufficient positive feedback to feel safe to move forward and close, or you will start hearing, feeling or seeing (through body language) some objections or concerns.

Typically, if you've done a thorough job going effectively from step 1 to step 7, you may be able to move straight to step 9 – closing. Indeed, that's the whole purpose of going through the steps, to avoid having objections when you try to close. The more experienced and competent you become on your sales journey, the fewer objections you're likely to encounter at the end. Objections are often a sign that you've missed something on the way. Sometimes objections just reflect a power-play in which the buyer wants to be awkward and express their authority before happily moving forward with you. Be careful not to lose it at this stage and get put off course.

## So what is an objection?

An objection in the sales process is a reason not to move forward. It is a barrier in the buyer's mind to closing a deal, or a reason to stall the decision because they aren't quite sure, or something's missing. It's the "Yes, *but*" or "I like you, *but*".

The best way to assess whether an objection is real or just a 'fob-off', is to look your buyer in the eye and ask "What if..." or "If...". In other words, remove the barrier hypothetically, allowing you to gauge reaction. Does the buyer seek another opt-out clause, which indicates there's more to this than originally stated, or do they convince you that it really is about this objection and therefore you need to find a way around it?

## Objections can be real or imaginary

**Real objections** are genuine, tangible or intangible reasons for stalling or not saying yes, for example:

*"I would like to order but your delivery time is too long."*

*"I like your product but it's not available with spots on!"*

*"You seem really nice and knowledgeable but I can only deal with companies who have the required accreditation."*

*"I'd love to buy but I don't have the budget this year."*

In the case of a real objection, your challenge is:

- to identify and understand it
- to see how critical it is in terms of blocking the sale; for example, if you can't get the product with 'spots on it', question whether it really matters, all else being equal;
- if it is a deal breaker, what can you do to resolve it, remove it or offer an alternative? Be creative and flexible – this is not necessarily about dropping your price but rather seeking a compromise in which they win and you win;
- to not give up or give in: seek ways forward, if not now, then for later (depending on the seriousness of the problem); try to keep the door and the dialogue open.

**Imaginary objections** are either made up (what could be termed smokescreens or lies) or perceived (the buyer sees something as an obstacle even though it isn't really, for example, a lack of confidence, previous history, fear).

In the case of smokescreens or lies, think about why the buyer would introduce this. Are they wanting to avoid the truth, confrontation or indeed making a decision? Typical smokescreens might be:

*"I need to ask my partner first."* (no, in reality, they don't; they have the ability to decide themselves);

*"I've no budget right now."* (actually in reality I have but I'd rather hold it back for something else);

*"I'm happy with my current supplier."* (actually they're not brilliant, but you're new and more of a risk)

## Examples of how to test objections

*"What if you had the budget... would you be happy to go ahead?"*

*"If it was down to you (and you didn't have to consult with your wife, or partner or...), how would you feel?"*

*"If we were able to do that for you in those timescales, in that colour, (or whatever the outlandish request)... would you be happy to place an order?"*

Once you have tested the objection and know that it's real, you can now handle and remove it. Don't try and move on before doing this, or it will come back to haunt you. If you brush it under the carpet, once you've left the room it will reappear and then you're not there to argue your case. Deal with all objections or concerns whilst you are in front of the buyer and make sure that every one of them has been resolved satisfactorily.

## Tips: Handling objections

**1** Be prepared – generally objections are predictable.

**2** Welcome objections by being open: "Tell me more!" In fact objections can be a sign of interest and buyer involvement.

**3** Seek first to understand – "I'd be interested to know why you think that?"

**4** Agree – "I can see where you're coming from...that's an interesting point of view."

**5** Don't be confrontational – don't get drawn into battle.

**6** Can it be resolved? Be creative: what alternatives can you offer?

**7** Is it important? Is it really a deal breaker or can it be parked?

**8** Unspoken objections must be flushed out – don't ignore them. If you feel something's up, then ask. Don't brush them aside or rush on.

**9** Never move on whilst an objection is still alive and festering or it will come back to haunt you. Deal with it fully.

**10** And finally, if you're not dealing with the decision-maker but rather the messenger, anticipate the decision-maker's objections and train your messenger to handle these on your behalf.

# Step 9     Gain commitment

You have now completed steps 1 to 3 *before* your meeting and steps 4 to 8 *during* the meeting and your prospect is really interested. You are getting positive buying signals, either verbalised or through body language.

Verbalised: *"That sounds good"; "I could really do with something like that"; "Spot on...!"*

Body language: gestures, eyes, smiling, nodding, posture.

This can happen at various points throughout your meeting. If so and it feels appropriate, close! Close when it's closable – don't ever feel the need to tell all just because you feel you should. Don't tell yourself, "I'm here now so I'll say what I came to say"! Take the business when it's being offered; you can sometimes bore the buyer out of a sale.

The key point about closing is to remember to close! Too many inexperienced sellers have numerous nice meetings with lots of nice people, drinking umpteen nice cups of coffee – but all this leads to no action or sales outcome. The whole purpose of the sales journey is to take your client from place A without you to place B with you. Now make it happen. Remember you agreed in step 4, when setting the purpose of the meeting, that if it makes sense, they'd do it – take action and buy!

---

**If B is a better place than A, and if the gains are greater than the cost of investment, then why not?**

---

Don't be shy, don't worry about rejection, and don't wait for the buyer to come back to you. This is not about being pushy; it's about stating clear facts and benefits and leading towards the final Logical Conclusion© – a sale.

## The Dos and Don'ts of closing

| DON'T | DO |
|---|---|
| Don't force a close – you can't close what's not closable. | Pick the right time; if it feels right, then go for it and close. |
| Don't forget to close – don't wait to be asked. | Take control – ask for the business if it makes sense. |
| Don't be vague and waffly; e.g. "I'll give you a call next week." | Close tightly and be clear on who does what – "I'll call you next Friday. Is 10am good for you?" |
| Don't leave the ball in the buyer's court, e.g. "I'll leave it with you for now. Call when you're ready." (They might never be!) | Be in control – agree you will take the next steps, when, how and what. |
| Don't assume they will call or email – they'll probably get busy and forget. | Summarise and get agreement on what happens next. Get commitment from the buyer on what they will do for you. |
| Don't try to close via a complex email proposal. | Arrange a follow-up meeting to present your proposal and get feedback face to face (if this makes commercial sense). |

Some closing statements or options:

- *"Based on this, I'd like to suggest we move things forward by agreeing some dates, quantities..."*

- *"That's great. A + B = C. How do you suggest we move this forward?"*

- *"That's great. A + B = C. How many would you like to order? When would you like to take delivery?"*

- *"Why don't we get things moving by completing the paperwork whilst I'm here, then I can get everything processed for you and we'll be ready to take your order as soon as..."*

- *"If I can take an order confirmation today, I can make sure you have delivery by the nth, which ties in nicely with the timescales you outlined!"*

- *"Let me check with the factory now (by phone) and see if we can slot that in for next week. If so, can I have your commitment to move things forward?"*

- *"Subject to me confirming everything in writing and clarifying those prices we discussed, shall we start looking at some dates for delivery and get a date pencilled in provisionally to work towards?"*

Choose whichever kind of statement is appropriate, given the way the meeting is going. The key is to create urgency without being pushy and to lead the buyer where they and you wish to go!

# 8

# The Post-meeting Phase

## Step 10 — Follow up

Follow up, follow up, follow up – I cannot emphasise this enough. One of the single biggest mistakes made by people new to sales is to not follow up effectively or indeed at all. This applies to every aspect of the sales process – follow up on proposals sent, follow up on telephone enquiries received, follow up on networking events attended. Never feel you've done enough by simply being there, showing up or giving information. Your challenge is to get the other person to take action as a result of your initial activity. You will only achieve this by taking or maintaining control through following up.

As a buyer and professional sales trainer, I am often stunned at how few people follow up on product information I have requested. This is an absolute waste! I find it incredible that a company would spend significant sums of money promoting their services so that you find them, in the first place, but then not follow up after you've made your initial inquiry.

Effective follow-up, once real need has been established, is *a service to the buyer* and in no way should you see this as hassling them!

## 5 common misconceptions and reasons for poor follow-up

1  You believe the buyer will do what they said they would.

2  You believe your job is now done; you've connected and you can leave it to the buyer to make up their mind, do what they promised, and get back to you; you move on to the next opportunity.

3  If you chase (too much), you might appear desperate, pushy or scare them off.

4  When they're ready, they'll get in touch

5  No other potential supplier (competitor) is involved or trying to win 'your deal' – you believe it's in the bag!

A few things to remember:

- It's *your* job to take the sale right through to its final conclusion – a sale is not a sale until money has changed hands. A verbal yes on the day is often just an expression of intent – it's what happens next that counts.

- Your buyer is busy and you may not be their number one priority. They may intend to follow up and get back to you but once you leave the room, they may get distracted or face other issues and challenges and you're quickly forgotten. You need to keep yourself on their radar.

- You are being unfair to the buyer and yourself by not following up and keeping the heat on! If you have closed effectively and you have both agreed the need and benefit, then you are depriving your buyer of your service by not making it happen. They have just got distracted, not necessarily disinterested. They need you to help them prioritise and make this happen. If your product adds value and makes a difference, they will thank you for this in the long-run.

## How to follow up effectively

### Make notes

Make notes during and after your meeting while what you need to record is still fresh in your mind. Be clear on what you have both agreed to do and plan what needs to happen next and when. Don't get distracted as you juggle a million balls in your new business venture. If you have a customer relationship management (CRM) system, put the notes and reminders into your system – see below.

### Do what you said you'd do

Do it really well and do it on time, as this will set the tone for what happens next. There's a golden rule in sales: 'under-promise and over-deliver'. Many sales people do the opposite and frustrate and alienate potential buyers. Get in touch with anyone else involved who needs to be aware of your commitments to the buyer and let them know what is required of them. Stick to deadlines you have set or advise your prospect if there's a problem or delay and explain the reason.

### Follow up immediately with a quick thank you note by email

Highlight the outcomes and remind your prospect of the key benefits you discussed. This is particularly important if your formal response will take some time. Keep things on the boil!

## Keep it going

Should the outcome of the meeting not result in an immediate opportunity, but you have agreed to stay in touch, then the ongoing follow-up is essential. Put these reminders into your diary, Outlook, or CRM system. Make notes on the frequency of contact, timing and preferred method to use. For some prospects this may be quite frequent, depending on the opportunity and level of activity. For others it may be a reminder to call in a year but to stay in touch via quarterly newsletter. You may wish to rank your prospects and follow up accordingly:

| | | |
|---|---|---|
| **Prospects A** | Excellent prospect – high value | Contact strategy: every 3-6 weeks |
| **Prospects B** | Reasonable prospect – average value | Contact strategy: 3-4 months |
| **Prospects C** | Poor prospect for now (may change) – low value | Contact strategy: once per year |

## Tip: Effective use of your time

All opportunities are not equal – make sure that you prioritise and time-manage your prospects accordingly and do not waste foolish amounts of time chasing low-value returns!

## Type of follow-up

### A second meeting

Always aim to have a follow-up meeting rather than emailing a proposal (unless this doesn't make commercial sense due to distance or size of opportunity). Once you email a document, you lose the ability to discuss and relate it to your original meeting outcomes. It's a fixed document – the communication is one-way! This may be alright in some situations but in others this is a cop-out and a lost opportunity to have another dialogue with your prospect. It's therefore important when you are closing your first meeting to aim to diarise this second appointment to discuss and tailor the proposal. Try talking about sharing ideas rather than writing a finished proposal. Focus on the outcome being collaborative, rather than directive.

### Proposal

If the prospect insists on sending through a proposal, or if you decide that this is the best or only way forward, then:

- Agree a date when you will ring for follow-up discussion on the proposal.

- Don't leave the ball in their court. Avoid saying, "Give me a ring when you've had a chance to look at it." This can drag on forever.

- Seek some commitment. You deserve it – you've invested time and energy into doing a proposal and you now deserve a dialogue. Make sure when you agree on doing a proposal that you set this out from the start by saying, for example, "I'm happy to go away and put some ideas together for you. I'll have these back to you by Friday... would Wednesday next week suit for a catch-up call to review your feedback and get your thoughts?" If they are not that keen, it will show at this point and you can assess whether preparing a proposal is worth your effort, or whether it will just go in the bin.

- Far too many sellers send information by post or by email without ever having a real commitment from the buyer. If this ends up in the bin, it shouldn't be a surprise. Challenge yourself as to whether this is a worthwhile outcome or whether you are letting the buyer off the hook with their fob-off – "Send me some prices through to have a look at".

- Be as specific as possible with your follow-up arrangements. What day should you call, at what time, on which contact number, and does anyone else need to be involved?

- Check out video-conferencing options if a second visit is not an option.

## Proposal content

For some contracts, especially in the public sector or larger organisations, the route to winning work is by submitting tenders. Normally in this situation there is a formal procedure and documentation to follow and 'sales meetings', as we have been discussing them in this book, are positively discouraged or even prohibited.

The type of proposal we're talking about here is a document prepared as follow-up to a sales meeting.

## Tips: Writing effective proposals

**1** Don't use a standard proposal. By all means have a standard format but think back to your meeting, your questioning, your matching, your agreed ROI, and then make sure your proposal reflects this and is not just a generic 'dump' which you could have sent to anyone, even if you hadn't met or talked to them.

**2** A proposal should not be confused with a quotation. Avoid sending just prices; they should have a clear link to the ROI and benefits discussed in your meeting.

**3** Make sure you clearly summarise your USPs and return on investment. Make it clear why they should pick you.

**4** Keep it short and clear; put any 'extra stuff' in appendices.

**5** Apply the 'YOU' test – would you read it if it landed on your desk? Does it look inviting? Is the cover boring and lack-lustre, or does it scream out to be opened and read?

**6** Think about the clear 'value' of what you're proposing. How will it impact significantly on this business or person – and is this clear from page one?

**7** Include evidence or proof of your work and testimonials which vouch for your track record.

**8** Make it relevant and specific to the industry sector. Don't talk in corporate language and use blue-chip company examples if it's aimed at a small business; don't talk about the breadth of your experience if the client is wanting an expert in a specific field and a more focused track record would convey this.

**9** Tailor, tailor, tailor – make the solution fit the need.

**10** Make sure that there is a clear 'call to action' so that the buyer knows exactly what to do next.

## A note about CRM systems

CRM refers to customer relationship management. For the purposes of this book, we are simply talking about a system which allows you to effectively manage data and activities in relation to customers and prospective customers. I am a big advocate of implementing an effective and simple CRM system to manage all your sales activity, right from the day you start your business. It should be your fountain of knowledge and a priceless asset. I am nervous and sceptical when people try to store all this knowledge in their head, or on bits or paper, or shove business cards into a drawer. A good system for storing information about your prospects – and ultimately your customers – will serve you well for life and will allow you to effectively manage all your sales activity and business relationships in an organised way.

I am not going to promote one system over another. Many of my clients use different systems – some off the shelf, some bespoke. It's really down to personal preference and specific needs. Some of the standard CRM software packages include ACT®, SalesLogix®, Goldmine® and Salesforce®, to mention but a few. It is worth exploring the market – you can pick up a single-user licence for relatively low cost.

### Why should you bother with a CRM?

- As your business and sales activity grows, you may struggle to manage your leads effectively.

- It sets a good discipline to be adopted later by any sales people you hire and avoids people storing vital sales data in their heads or personal storage systems. When a sales person moves on, you have that vital information in a central place. (Words of warning however: Be careful about who can access and copy your data and check about compliance with the Data Protection Act.).

- It allows you to manage your follow-up activity and prompts you very effectively to stay in touch.

- It gives you an excellent overview of your sales pipeline and allows you to forecast potential sales revenue.

- It allows you to track your individual sales successes and overall performance ratios and also to evaluate the ROI from different marketing activities. It allows you to analyse what is yielding the best return in terms of sales leads, appointments and sales value.

- You'd be silly not to – at the start it's an easy discipline. As your business grows, it becomes a more difficult and onerous task (but arguably, more crucial, too)

- It allows you to develop the basis for an effective e-marketing or direct mail strategy based on your personal database, rather than buying-in data from list sellers.

# Step 11    Review performance and celebrate

Whether you win it or lose it, review it!

Particularly in the early stages of your sales experience it's vital to reflect on your sales meetings by asking yourself:

- What worked? – What would I repeat and why?

- What didn't work? – What did I miss? What lessons have I learned?

The key thing is to review, refine and improve your performance. Make notes and look at these before your next meeting. Selling is partly an art and partly a science – and you get better by practising over and over again.

If things aren't going well and you're not getting results, ask yourself why. What could you have done differently? Review steps 1 to 10 – did you do them? Did you miss any? Was something not right along the way?

You will often hear that sales is a numbers game and that you can't win all the time. It's true, but the important thing is to learn from each situation.

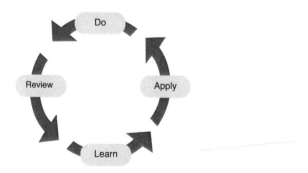

Be clear on why – why no and why yes!

**Why NO?**

| | |
|---|---|
| **Not today or not now** | Put the details into your CRM and revisit again. |
| **Not me 'prospect'** | Wrong company or wrong audience or not the right person. |
| **Not you 'seller'** | You didn't click, didn't say or do the right thing. Try again or get someone else to try (if that's an option). |
| **Don't need** | Either they didn't understand, didn't 'get' it or had no need. But is it just now or never? Eliminate or reassign the contact in your CRM. |

Examine every no and decide what should happen next, when, by whom and how. What have you learned? Don't repeat the same mistakes over and over again.

Remember the definition of insanity:

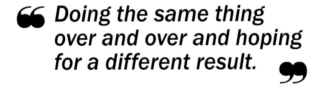

## *Doing the same thing over and over and hoping for a different result.*

If it's not working, change it – try a different audience, a different industry sector, a different message, time it differently! But don't give up.

## Why YES?

Yes is fabulous. You've won; you've succeeded; you've got the business and won a new client. Why? – was it just luck or was it:

$$\underset{\textbf{you}}{\text{Right}} + \underset{\textbf{client}}{\text{Right}} + \underset{\textbf{product}}{\text{Right}} + \underset{\textbf{process}}{\text{Right}} + \underset{\textbf{tenacity}}{\text{Right}} = \textbf{SALE}$$

Examine the formula – *your* personal Winning Sales Formula – to understand what worked and repeat it. Where are there more of the same kinds of problems and the same kinds of people who need your solution? Where else can you add value? How will you connect with these other people, and what will your key message be? Now go for it and win!

If you've won new business as a result of your sales meeting success, well done! You've made it, so give yourself a big pat on the back. Celebrate your victory in some way; often we are the first to beat ourselves up when things go wrong, so make sure you big yourself up when things go right. If others were involved in helping win the sale, let them know and share the victory. Selling can be tough, so maximise on the good times and positive results. Harness this positive energy – now is the best time to look for opportunity number two.

# Step 12   Maximise the opportunity

So you've now won a customer, perhaps your first. You've put all of the pieces of the sales formula logically together and you've got someone to commit to doing business with you. That was the hard bit. The easy bit is now getting the best possible return on your time invested in sales. Your aim is to maximise your ROI and theirs. I've said it's easy and I promise you it is. The fact that very few people actually do this properly is because:

- they are too busy chasing the next deal

- they are too busy working in the business (not on the business)

- they are too complacent (they sit back and think the customer will continue to come back to them)

- they are too afraid of being pushy

- they are too focused on one specific 'small' opportunity, rather than looking at the big picture.

We will look at the 'too busy' arguments in chapter 9, but for now focus on the ways in which you can get maximum return on investment (ROI) from your sales and marketing time and money.

Maximising ROI hinges around understanding the value of each customer to your business in quantifiable sales terms. Does a customer buy one product once and then you never see them again, or are you truly maximising their potential and value to your business over a lifetime? We call this the Lifetime Value (LTV) of a customer.

There are five important strategies for maximising on the lifetime value of a customer (not every strategy will apply to every customer but they are all worth considering):

# 5 simple strategies for maximising LTV

1 Cross-selling: *"Would you like fries with that?"*

2 Upselling: *"Twice the price, three times the value!"*

3 Updating: *"You might like to know that...?"*

4 Cross-dating: *"Is there anyone else who...?"*

5 Top-dating: *"Just thinking of you!"*

**Cross-selling (sometimes called link selling)**

Let me be clear: cross-selling is not about pushing unwanted additional product onto your customer; it is about advising them what else you do that complements what they have just purchased and which would provide additional benefit to them. It is wrong to assume that they already know or might guess what else you could offer them – they might, but then again they might not! Your job is to communicate clearly what else you offer, and explain any additional benefits. By not letting customers know what else they can easily buy from you, you are in fact letting them down: you are depriving them of an opportunity to save time, hassle, inconvenience, cost, etc.

A typical example would be selling a toy at Christmas that requires a battery and not asking "Would you like batteries to go with that?" Think of the kid's disappointment when they unwrap their present and can't play with it because 'batteries not included'. The key is to think laterally and see yourself as assisting the buyer – advise your customer on what else they might need to make life easier, better or smoother. You are doing them and yourself a disservice by not making the relevant connections or links.

**Upselling**

Upselling is about increasing the value of a purchase or selling up. Instead of the customer buying a cheap version of a product, you recommend a more expensive version which ultimately represents better value to the customer. I firmly believe in selling with integrity, and the latter point is important if you, too, are committed to ethical selling. Upselling is not about ripping off the customer and trying to sell them a more expensive option they don't need; it's about understanding the customer's need and how a solution addresses that need, and then advising if there is a more suitable item that would do the job better, or that would perhaps last longer. Again, don't assume that the customer knows what is best – they may just be asking for what they have always asked for. Your job is to educate and explain to them the benefits of spending more money with you by describing the net impact and ultimate saving or benefit for them in terms of time, money, their happier customers, etc. You are simply helping your customer to buy well.

## Updating

It's important in sales to regularly update your clients about new products and services, product improvements, new people, processes and skills in your business. Particularly if you're just starting in business, you'll be growing, developing, and learning all the time, so share this knowledge with your clients on a regular basis. It is far cheaper and far easier to sell new products and services to existing clients, than to find new ones; you simply need to invest the time in updating them.

Focus on regularly re-connecting with your customers and exploring ways in which you can add value to their business; think about what else you can do for them. Don't just dump information on them – make sure it's relevant and specific to their needs and that 'they get' what it does for them (review chapter 4 on your product). Choose a variety of communication methods, from telephone catch-up to sit-down meetings, e-zines to blogs, etc. Don't just stick to one method and bore people or hassle them to death!

For sales success, communication needs to be clear, frequent and varied – so that eventually your customer 'gets it'. Remember 'The 7 to 11 Rule' (page 55). Don't fall at the first hurdle just because you get a no. It might be that they just haven't heard properly, your timing is wrong, they don't get it or simply that they haven't got around to placing their order...yet! Get proactive and reconnect.

## Cross-dating

Cross-dating, also known as networking, is all about how you maximise on the positive relationships you have with your customers and how you cross-fertilise.

## Tips: Cross-dating

**1** Seek and you will find. Don't wait for referrals and recommendations to come to you – they may and that's great. However, many people aren't naturally proactive so you need to let them know the sort of referrals you're looking for and ask them to recommend you to their colleagues, friends, family – the audience that is specifically relevant to you. If they like you and are happy with your service they will be pleased to do this.

**2** 'Shy bairns get nowt!' Ask "who else?" "where else?" – "Which other department or person or company do you know where you feel I could add value?" 'Who should I speak with or ask for?' "Would you be happy to make the initial introduction." Ask, ask, ask!

**3** Minimise the need to cold-call by getting warm introductions. Think about who you might want to connect with and review your network and customer base to explore who would be happy to make an initial introduction.

### Top-dating

Who makes the best dates, the best friends, the best lovers? They usually are the ones that make you feel great about yourself! They communicate regularly; they're there when you need them; they put you and your needs first; they tell you they love you; they remember your birthday; they maybe even bring you flowers and champagne.

Consider how you 'top date' your customers and prospects or how you stay 'top of their mind'. Remember that the first sale is just a trial and that they are just trying you out. You have to look after, nurture and protect your customers, or they may run off with someone else. Real, sustainable sales success and repeat business will come if you remember to tell your customers regularly that they matter and that you care. Utilise your marketing and ongoing communication skills to support your hard-won initial sales and drive up your ROI. Your business will thrive as a result.

# Part Three

---

# A Lifetime Habit

# 9

# Selling – a Quick Fix or a Lifetime Habit?

Before concluding, let me share with you some sales challenges I see business owners face as their businesses grow and the demand and pressure on their time increases.

## 1 Selling needs to be a lifetime habit, not a quick fix

Many small business owners see selling as a quick fix, rather than a lifetime habit: "When things are quiet, I'll do a bit of selling." The worst time to look for business is when you're quiet, because this usually means you're needy and desperate and very often it's a case of too little, too late. Little and often, even when you appear not to need it, is truly best practice.

## 2 Selling needs to be proactive, not reactive

Once you start winning customers there is a danger that you sit back and wait for the rest to follow. This is usually because we're busy and not because we're lazy. There is a double danger here: first the flood of customers may not happen, or if it does, then possibly not to the levels and timescales required; second the business that comes to you may not be the business you want!

Now you might have the sort of business where you say "I'll take anything that comes my way" (and that might be acceptable in cases such as certain retail or online businesses) but be careful of the 'busy fool syndrome'. Are you busy making very little money from the wrong kind of customers? Could you make more money, work less hard, and be paid quicker with a different type of customer? If you're clear on the kind of customer you want, get proactive and find them. Don't wait and hope they'll find you.

## 3 Success is dependent on the time you invest in the process

Quality input brings quality output. Set your goal and determine what you need to invest to reach that goal. Whether you want one, or a hundred, new customers a year, a month, a week or a day, consider how much time it takes to identify, connect with, meet with and convert each prospect, and how much wastage may occur along the way. Initially it will be trial and error, but measure your input and if it isn't generating the right output, something needs changing – the amount of time invested, the source or type of lead, or the sales skills applied. The key thing is to put a certain (agreed) amount of time in your diary for proactive selling, i.e., connecting (chapter 5), and don't let anything get in the way or distract you.

## 4 How can I sell more without hiring sales people?

In the early days especially, and indeed throughout your business journey, it's vital that you are not the only person bringing in sales. How can you create a bigger sales team without hiring? Consider who else in your business, family or network could sell on your behalf by identifying opportunities, making connections and introductions and bringing in the business.

It's vital as your business grows and you take on other staff that they too recognise their contributory role in the sales process. Everyone in a business (especially a small business) needs to be tuned in to sales and recognise their input and value. Equally you need to quickly identify and tackle any anti-sales culture and 'sales prevention people' or departments where people see sales, orders and customers as a problem, rather than the valuable lifeblood of the business.

## 5 How do I hire good sales people?

At some stage, sooner or later, you may identify that you are not the best, or the only person, to sell in your business and that you need to hire a dedicated sales person. Do so with great care. Be clear who and what you're looking for and make sure you do your homework before hiring. Recommendation is important, as is proven track record. Don't fall for someone who has the 'gift of the gab' or that you simply bump into. Remember we discovered earlier that great selling is about much more – it's is about two-way connections with people. Always be on the look-out for someone you think can add value to your sales team – someone with focus, passion and drive. They're out there but not always the easiest to find. Poor sales people can be a very costly mistake and detrimental to your brand. Plan to get it right.

## 6 How do I keep my 'mojo'?

When starting a new business, you're probably full of enthusiasm and passion, really excited about what the future holds and ready to work your socks off to achieve it. For some, maintaining this high level of motivation is easy and comes naturally; for others it's harder, and when the going gets tough and there is a series of knock-backs, morale can dip.

Finding and keeping your mojo is vital in business and even more so in sales where rejection is inevitable. Mojo is Motivation and Joy – the passion, inspiration and fun in what you do. This is infectious and will draw others to you and your business. Displaying, or allowing others to see, the opposite, or lack of mojo, will drive people away. Keeping your mojo is about:

- Focusing on your original motivation – Why are you doing what you're doing? – What was your original vision and inspiration?

- Keeping your eye on the prize – What will be the reward or prize if you achieve your goals? Is this exciting and motivational? Does it perhaps guarantee security or peace of mind?

- Surrounding yourself with the right people who inspire and motivate you, rather than bring you down

- Taking time out for yourself, your loved ones, your hobbies – recharge your batteries or they'll go dead

- Learning, growing, thriving – everything you do in life will teach you something. See every learning experience as unique and special to you. Learn to embrace the good, the bad and the ugly. You and your business will be better as a result

- Finally – above all else, having a clear set of objectives and a clear plan. "If you don't know where you are going, any road will get you there."[†] But if you do, then some simple planning will help you reach your destination in the most effective way and help preserve your mojo.

Download and use the Sales Development Plan template to help with your business development plan.

**www.winningsales.co.uk/resources**
···→ Sales Development Plan

[†] Lewis Carroll, *Alice in Wonderland*

# **10** lifetime principles of great selling

1 Just do it! Always have your sales antennae switched on and never be too busy for sales.

2 No is fine... it's not personal and a yes is around the corner. Keep your head up, and keep going.

3 Surround yourself with positive people who encourage and motivate. Selling is tough so don't make it worse by having negative 'I told you so' people in the background.

4 Believe in yourself, your product, your service, your value. Be clear on what makes you special – what's your little bit of magic?

5 Sell with integrity if you're trying to build a long-term, sustainable business. Short-term gain can lead to long-term pain.

6 Process + passion = success; process alone is not enough.

7 Seek always to understand your customer, prospect, buyer. See yourself as an 'assistant buyer' – help your buyer to buy well and preferably from you.

8 Value you and your time – be equal to your buyer, not their underdog. Seek win–win in all situations. Don't beg, grovel or be too desperate for a deal. Be proud, stand strong and negotiate.

9 Develop the habit of lifelong learning – you can always learn and improve – seek continuous opportunities to upskill your sales talents.

10 Recharge, re-energise, reward – take time out. Vitality, energy and passion are key to success. Reward yourself, reward others – it's tough out there so don't forget to say "Well done and thanks" – to yourself, your staff, your customers.

# Conclusion

Before I sign off, a few parting words.

I have thoroughly enjoyed sharing with you my Winning Sales Formula for selling success. I hope that you too will have an equal measure of success and fun in applying, adapting and honing this newly acquired knowledge. If you are taking your first steps into selling with this book, then I'm guessing that many of the concepts will be new, so please avoid trying to do too much too soon. Take a step-by-step approach and revisit each chapter as you encounter the trials and tribulations of the real world of selling. Success is inevitable, but not necessarily instantaneous. Try little and often, until it becomes that vital, lifetime habit.

Remember, this book is about *what it takes*, not just *how to do it*. Based on my experiences in sales, what it takes (the will-set) is actually more important than how to do it (the skill-set). A positive mental attitude and desire to succeed, coupled with *some* fundamental knowledge and skill, will always outperform the reluctant well-read sales theorist waiting for perfection before taking the plunge. The time for selling is now; the time for learning and fine-tuning is ongoing.

So go for it! If you are to make a success of your new business venture and succeed in a very noisy, cluttered marketplace, effective selling is key. Believe in yourself, your product and service and seek to connect with those out there who need you, trying out your newly acquired knowledge as you go. If you have something of value to offer, your new customers will thank you for your tenacity in the end. Remember, if they don't know you exist they can't buy, so it's up to you. Get proactive and get selling – today.

I wish you successful selling, a thriving business and lots of happy customers.


*PS. Don't forget to let me know how you get on.*
*Email me at **jackie@winningsales.co.uk**, tweet **@winningsales** or leave your comments on my website **www.winningsales.co.uk***

# Sales Jargon Buster

**Active need (page 27)**

A need, problem or pain which has been identified or recognised by a customer or prospect (the opposite being dormant need - see below).

**Closing (pages 5, 8, 22, 27, 61, 66, 94-96)**

Closing a sale refers to achieving a clearly defined, tangible and mutually agreed final outcome between buyer and seller, either a sale or agreed next step.

**Closed question (pages 79, 89)**

A question which can be answered by one word: Yes, No, Maybe, Sometimes, Never.

**Cold-calling (page 50)**

Telephone selling or calling to prospects where there is no previous track record or relationship.

**Cross-selling (pages 61, 109, 131)**

Selling an additional product (or products) which naturally links or fits with the original purchase.

**CRM system (pages 100, 101, 105, 107)**

A Customer Relationship Management system is an IT solution for storing, managing and tracking data about your customers and prospects.

**Dormant need (pages 27, 28)**

The opposite of active need (see above) – a need which has not yet been identified or recognised by the customer. The seller may have identified the need but the buyer isn't yet aware of their need.

**Gatekeeper (page 54)**

Someone who may be the interface or barrier to your ultimate decision-maker. Likely to be a PA or secretary or receptionist.

**Lifetime Value (LTV) (pages 22, 59, 61, 109)**

In relation to a customer, this is the value of the customer to a business over the customer's lifetime with that business.

### Link selling (page 109)

Linking two product sales together. A customer buys one thing and you introduce something else that naturally links to the first purchase (see cross-selling).

### Lead (page 117)

An unqualified prospect. Someone you think may have a need but you now need to qualify it.

### Objection (page 66, 89, 91, 93)

A barrier or obstacle to closing a sale; a customer's reason (stated or implied, real or imagined) for possibly not moving forward.

### Opportunity (pages 65-69, 101, 108-109)

A qualified piece of potential business from a new prospect or existing customer.

### Open questions (pages 79, 89)

Questions beginning with who, what, where, when, how, why and which and that cannot be answered with yes, no or another one-word answer. Seeks to gain a more detailed response.

### Pain (pages 37, 54)

A problem or need that the customer has which makes him uncomfortable and needs to be addressed or requires a solution.

### Pipeline (pages 23, 105)

In the context of sales, this refers to the prospects you are in contact with at different stages of interest and who are in line to be converted, at some stage, into future customers.

### Prospect (pages 19, 21, 24...)

A potential customer – someone you have identified as having a need you can fulfil.

### TLC (page 23)

Tender Loving Care; not specifically a sales term but used in the context of this book to remind you of the need to treat all your customers as lovers and friends and to look after them well, or else you run the risk of losing them.

**ROI - Return on Investment (page 16, 43, 87)**

A financial accountancy term which in the context of this book looks at the return on investment the customer gets by buying a particular product or service.

**Upselling (page 110)**

Increasing the value of the sale upwards by selling a higher value item.

**USP (pages 40, 78)**

Unique Selling Point or Proposition – what makes you stand out from the crowd.

# Acknowledgements

Since that wonderful day when I was commissioned to write this book, so many people have helped, inspired, encouraged and nurtured me along the way. To all of you, my heartfelt thanks and gratitude.

I would especially like to thank:

Jan Jones who spent half her holiday in the UK lovingly doing that first crucial edit. You have been a loving aunt and wonderful friend throughout my career and indeed my life. Judith Mashiter, who took over as the professional editor and knew how to carefully craft and kept the pressure on right to the end. Jerri Murtagh, my young and gifted PR agent and friend – thank you for understanding the realities of my world and all the juggling, both physical and mental – you always make every decision I take okay, even when I turned down that big PR moment for my daughter's prom!

A big thanks to all at Brightword Publishing. It has been wonderful working with you all. Especial thanks to Louise Hinchen, Suzanne Anderson and of course the amazing Emma Jones, with all her vision and passion to create an amazing business. Thanks for taking a chance on me and being so flexible in our undertakings together – a real partnership.

Thanks to Jayne Graham and Michelle Gudgeon for spotting that first 'tweet' – it may not have happened without you. To all those who read those early manuscripts and whose suggestions and contributions were invaluable, including Martin Lloyd-Penny, Helen Butler, Clare Adamson and her team at Newcastle University. Also those who reviewed the first eBook in the early days and gave great feedback and encouragement – Derek Curtis, Jayson Guernsey, Rob Richardson, Guy Letts and many more.

And finally to my team at home – Keith, Emily, Hannah and Michael. I love you all and thank you for keeping me sane and supporting me along this sometimes fraught journey. I hope I managed to juggle most of the balls (at least the important ones) and thanks to Keith for catching the ones I almost dropped! You all make me immensely proud.

*Jackie Wade*
*November 2011*

# About Jackie Wade

Jackie Wade is the petite and passionate sales dynamo from Dublin. Committed to ethical and professional selling practises, Jackie is focused on helping businesses succeed in highly competitive marketplaces.

Jackie's love affair with sales and selling began when, aged 6, she took charge of the "sweetie department" in her grandmother's corner shop in Ireland and soon discovered the excitement and independence of earning some real pocket money. Helping to run a number of market stalls around Dublin's fair city through her teenage years was to provide a tough but very valuable insight into buying and selling and working with people from all walks of life. After studying International Marketing & Languages, Jackie went on to pursue a global career in International Sales and Marketing, developing business in places as far flung as the USA, Australia and South America.

In 2000, following the birth of her twins, Jackie decided to park her corporate heels and set up her own business in sales training, coaching and sales strategy. In 2004, Winning Sales was born. In just a few short years, Jackie has become a highly sought-after trainer, motivational speaker, business coach and guest on numerous radio shows and business panels. Jackie has an impressive portfolio of private clients from football's premiership boardrooms to top universities and law firms. She also supports diverse business start-up and social enterprise initiatives around the UK and is passionate about helping people overcome their fears and inhibitions when it comes to selling their products and services, generating growth and creating wealth.

Whether as a trainer, coach or motivational speaker, Jackie's Irish charm and self-deprecating humour, knowledgeable content and memorable case studies all serve to inspire and motivate audiences of all backgrounds around the globe.

**For more information on the services and training programmes Winning Sales offers, please visit www.winningsales.co.uk**

# About Brightword Publishing

Brightword Publishing is a new venture from Harriman House and Enterprise Nation. Brightword produce print books, kits and digital products aimed at a small business and start up audience, providing high-quality information from high-profile experts in an accessible and approachable way.

## Our other Business Bites

**Pitching Products for Small Business: How to successfully prepare your business, brand and products, and sell to retail buyers**

by Laura Rigney

eBook ISBN: 978-0-85719-041-3
Print ISBN: 978-1-90800-317-1

**The Small Business Guide to China: How small enterprises can sell their goods or services to markets in China**

by David Howell

eBook ISBN: 978-1-908003-11-9
Print ISBN: 978-1-908003-22-5

**Successful Selling for Small Business: What It Takes and How To Do It**

by Jackie Wade

eBook ISBN: 978-1-90800-308-9
Print ISBN: 978-1-908003-19-5

### Contracts for Small Business: A straightforward guide to contracts and legal agreements

by Charles Boundy

eBook ISBN: 978-1-908003-16-4
Print ISBN: 978-1-908003-21-8

### Finance for Small Business: A straight-talking guide to finance and accounting

by Emily Coltman

eBook ISBN: 978-1-90800-306-5
Print ISBN: 978-1-908003-20-1

# Other products from Brightword

49 Quick Ways to Market your Business for Free: An instant guide to marketing success

by Sarah-Jane White

eBook ISBN: 978-0-85719-144-1

50 Fantastic Franchises!: The UK's Best Franchise and Direct Selling Opportunities for Small Businesses

by Emma Jones and Sarah Clay

eBook ISBN: 978-1-90800-302-7

Go Global: How to Take Your Business to the World

by Emma Jones

Print ISBN: 978-1-90800-300-3
eBook ISBN: 978-1-90800-303-4

Motivating Business Mums: Inspiration, ideas and advice from 45 small business owners

by Debbie O'Connor

eBook ISBN: 978-1-90800-309-6

**The Start-Up Kit: Everything you need to start a small business**

by Emma Jones

ISBN: 978-1-90800-301-0

**Little Black Business Books - Networking Step By Step: A guide to making networking work for you**

by Marilyn Messik

eBook ISBN: 978-1-908003-14-0

**Little Black Business Books - Setting Up and Growing Your Business**

by Marilyn Messik

eBook ISBN: 978-1-908003-15-7

**Little Black Business Books - Getting Your Business Message Across: A guide to common-sense business communication**

by Marilyn Messik

eBook ISBN: 978-1-90800-325-6